ADA CARTIANU

THE ETHICS OF MINDFUL POLITICS

Building Equitable Political Systems

THE ETHICS OF MINDFUL POLITICS
Building Equitable Political Systems

Our book may be purchased in bulk for educational use.
Please contact your local book seller, Barnes & Noble, Amazon,
IngramSpark, RebELLE P.A or Ada Cartianu Art Gallery at
office@adacartianu.com
www.AdaCartianu.com

TABLE OF CONTENTS

INTRODUCTION

In a world grappling with deep divides, where the values of democracy, diversity, and inclusivity are often reduced to political slogans or mere ideals, the need for a profound and mindful approach to politics has never been greater. *The Ethics of Mindful Politics: Building Equitable Political Systems* is a call to rethink how we engage with one another in the realm of governance. It is a challenge to transcend partisan gridlock and exclusionary practices, to rebuild systems rooted not just in legal frameworks, but in empathy, respect, and genuine acceptance.

At the heart of mindful politics is the belief that democracy is more than a system of voting—it is a living, breathing entity that thrives when every voice is heard, every individual is valued, and every perspective is acknowledged. True democracy does not flourish in the shadows of fear and divisiveness; it rises in the light of collaboration and shared understanding. This book is a journey through that light—offering the principles and practices needed to foster a more inclusive, equitable, and compassionate political landscape.

Through this exploration, we will ask: How can we cultivate political spaces where all are not only invited but truly belong? How can we build systems that elevate our shared humanity, rather than diminish it? *The Ethics of Mindful Politics* seeks to uncover the ethical foundations necessary for constructing political systems that are as diverse and dynamic as the people they serve, and as just and harmonious as the society we aspire to create.

This is more than theory—it is a roadmap for a democracy that goes beyond the ballot box, a guide to creating lasting, meaningful change through mindful action, understanding, and collective responsibility. This is a call to transform politics from the inside out, to make it more than just a mechanism of governance, but a true reflection of the diverse, inclusive, and accepting world we envision.

In the heart of democracy lies a profound paradox: the pursuit of collective freedom must balance the very real needs and voices of every individual within it. **The Ethics of Mindful Politics** is an invitation to rethink and redefine political systems—not just as mechanisms of governance, but as living, breathing expressions of our shared humanity. In a world that is increasingly struggling with political systems to recognize the beauty and complexity of diversity, we are called to build political structures that are more than merely functional; they must be transformative, inclusive, and attuned to the deep currents of social justice and equity.

This book does not offer a one-size-fits-all solution or easy answers. Instead, it presents a vision—rooted in mindfulness and ethics—that seeks to create spaces where all voices are not only heard but truly listened to. It advocates for a democracy that doesn't just tolerate diversity but actively celebrates it; a system that accepts and learns from difference, rather than fearing it.

Crucial to this reimagining are considerations of how to safeguard against the rise of autocratic and oligarchic systems. The book examines the ethical implications of power concentration, the erosion of democratic institutions, and the manipulation of information, exploring how to build robust systems that are resilient to such threats.

We are living in times that demand profound change, where the call for inclusion, acceptance, and the recognition of human dignity has never been more urgent. *The Ethics of Mindful Politics* explores the complex interplay of these ideals, asking how we can build political systems that reflect the full range of human experiences, foster trust, and center equity at every level of decision-making.

It is time for politics to be more than a system of rules and procedures. It is time for politics to be a practice of deep empathy, mutual respect, and intentional connection. The journey toward a more equitable, inclusive, and just political landscape begins with understanding the profound responsibility we all share in shaping it. Through mindfulness, reflection, and a commitment to ethical principles, we can forge a political future that honors both the individual and the collective, with compassion, care, and consciousness at its core.

In this book, we will explore how to create political systems that not only embrace difference but are also capable of transforming power structures to reflect the true values of democracy. We will examine the ways in which mindfulness can help us reimagine politics—not as a game of winners and losers, but as a collective project of building a more just and equitable world for all.

This book is a tribute to those who, despite the possibility of authoritarianism and the allure of oligarchic power, continue to believe in the enduring strength of democracy. It is for those who understand that the fight for justice is never easy, but always necessary.

In the face of oppressive systems, we must recognize the beauty and power of our collective diversity—of thought, of background, of experience. It is through this diversity that we find the solutions to our most pressing challenges and the courage to stand against those who would silence us. Unity does not mean uniformity, but rather the strength found in our differences when we come together with a common purpose: *the preservation and flourishing of freedom.*

May this book inspire you to continue the struggle, knowing that every voice, no matter how small, contributes to the larger fight for a just, democratic world. Let hope be our guiding light, and may we never forget that the power to create change lies within all of us, when we unite in the pursuit of truth and justice.

With deep respect and unwavering hope for the future,

Ada Cartianu

EMBRACING UCONVENTIONAL PHILOSOPHIES FOR SOCIAL CHANGE

THE ESSENCE OF DEMOCRACY

Defining Democracy in Contemporary Terms

Democracy, in contemporary terms, transcends the simplistic notion of electoral processes and political representation. It embodies a dynamic interplay between individual agency and collective aspirations, where each voice contributes to the larger narrative of social change. This redefined understanding invites us to consider democracy not merely as a system of governance but as a living philosophy that nourishes our desire for fulfillment, equality, and justice. By embracing unconventional philosophies, we can cultivate a democracy that resonates with our deepest values and the innate structures of humanity.

At the heart of this reimagined democracy lies the principle of individual agency. Each person's capacity to influence their environment is crucial in shaping social movements that challenge the status quo. This empowerment fosters a sense of responsibility and ownership over the societal landscape. When individuals assert their rights and act in alignment with their values, they not only reshape their own lives but also inspire others to join the struggle for a more just and equitable society. This ripple effect underscores the importance of personal commitment in the broader context of activism and reform.

Non-conformity plays a pivotal role in the evolution of political systems, often serving as a catalyst for change. Those who dare to question established norms and challenge prevailing ideologies illuminate pathways toward alternative possibilities. This act of dissent, while sometimes met with resistance, can ignite conversations that lead to transformative outcomes. By embracing a mindset that celebrates diversity of thought and action, we can dismantle oppressive structures and foster an environment where radical ideas flourish, paving the way for a democracy that serves all members of society.

The intersection of existentialism and political activism offers profound insights into the human condition and our collective quest for meaning. In a world where mainstream narratives often suppress individuality, existentialist thought encourages us to confront the absurdities of existence and assert our freedom. This philosophical lens empowers us to engage politically while remaining true to ourselves, allowing for authentic expressions of dissent and advocacy. By aligning our personal fulfillment with community well-being, we craft a political landscape that honors both the individual and the collective.

Ultimately, the reimagination of democracy hinges on the ethics of dissent, mindfulness, and the pursuit of happiness within the framework of social justice.

As we navigate the complexities of modern life, cultivating a mindful approach to political engagement can deepen our understanding of the interconnectedness of our struggles. By nurturing a culture that values ethical dissent and embraces alternative lifestyles, we cultivate not only a more vibrant democracy but also a society that aligns with our innate desire for a fulfilling existence. Through these unconventional lenses, we can inspire a profound transformation that honors our shared humanity and the quest for a better world.

THE HISTORICAL CONTEXT OF DEMOCRATIC THOUGHT

Democratic thought has evolved through centuries, shaped by a rich interplay of philosophical ideas and social movements that reflect humanity's quest for a more just and equitable society. From the ancient Greek philosophers who first pondered the essence of governance and individual agency, to the Enlightenment thinkers who championed rights and freedoms, the historical context of democratic thought reveals a tapestry woven with the threads of dissent, innovation, and the relentless pursuit of fulfillment. In this exploration, we unearth the foundational principles that have not only influenced political systems but have also resonated deeply with our inner desires for connection, meaning, and the ability to shape our destinies.

The roots of democratic thought can be traced back to the philosophical inquiries of figures like Socrates, Plato, and Aristotle, who laid the groundwork for understanding democracy as more than a mere system of governance. Their discussions emphasized the importance of the individual in relation to the state, arguing that true fulfillment arises from active participation in civic life. These early reflections underscore the notion that personal agency is central to social change, a theme that continues to inspire contemporary movements advocating for justice and equality. By embracing our roles as active participants rather than passive spectators, we reclaim our power to influence the world around us.

As history progressed, the Enlightenment brought forth a radical shift in the perception of individual rights and the role of reason in politics. Thinkers like John Locke and Jean-Jacques Rousseau expanded the conversation about democracy, asserting that governmental authority must derive from the consent of the governed. This era marked a significant departure from traditional hierarchies, fostering a spirit of non-conformity that challenged oppressive systems. The legacy of these revolutionary ideas empowers individuals today to engage in civil disobedience and dissent, advocating for systemic change in a society that often contradicts our intrinsic values and ethical imperatives.

In the 20th century, existentialist philosophers like Jean-Paul Sartre and Simone de Beauvoir further enriched the discourse by intertwining personal fulfillment with political activism. They posited that authentic existence is tied to the struggle against oppression, urging individuals to confront societal norms that stifle their potential. This intersection of philosophical thought and activism invites us to reflect on our own lives and the collective journeys we undertake toward a more equitable society. By embracing alternative lifestyles and rejecting mainstream conformity, we assert our right to happiness and fulfillment, fostering communities that honor diverse expressions of identity and purpose.

Reimagining democracy through unconventional perspectives requires a deep understanding of the ethical implications of our actions. As we engage with mindfulness and cultivate awareness, we recognize the profound relationship between personal fulfillment and community well-being. This understanding inspires us to participate in social movements not merely as a means to an end but as a holistic approach to living in alignment with our values. By drawing on the wisdom of ancient philosophies and integrating these lessons into our modern struggles, we can envision a democracy that not only serves the needs of the many but also honors the richness of the human experience, ultimately leading us toward a brighter and more fulfilling future.

REIMAGINING DEMOCRACY
Fresh Perspectives on Democratic Practices

In the quest for a more fulfilling and just society, fresh perspectives on democratic practices emerge as essential catalysts for both individual and collective transformation. Traditional democratic frameworks often fall short in addressing the complexities of human nature and the diverse aspirations of individuals. By embracing unconventional philosophies, we can reimagine democracy as a living, breathing entity that evolves alongside the people it serves. This approach not only acknowledges the unique desires of individuals but also fosters a deeper connection to the common good, allowing for a more vibrant and inclusive society.

The role of individual agency in social movements cannot be overstated. Each person's choices and actions contribute to the larger tapestry of societal change. When individuals are empowered to express their unique perspectives, they challenge the status quo and inspire others to do the same. This ripple effect can lead to profound shifts in political systems, revealing the power of non-conformity as a driving force for innovation and reform. By valuing each person's contribution, we create a democratic space that honors diversity and encourages active participation, ultimately enriching the democratic process itself.

Existentialism offers a compelling lens through which to view political activism. It reminds us that our existence precedes essence, suggesting that individuals have the power to define their own paths and values. This philosophy aligns seamlessly with the pursuit of social justice, encouraging citizens to engage deeply with their beliefs and take responsibility for their actions. When individuals connect their personal fulfillment to the broader narrative of social change, they become agents of transformation, using their unique voices to advocate for a more equitable society. This intersection of personal meaning and political engagement breathes new life into democratic practices.

Alternative lifestyles serve as powerful expressions of dissent against mainstream societal norms. By choosing to live differently, individuals challenge entrenched power structures and inspire others to question the status quo. These unconventional choices often lead to innovative solutions and community-building efforts that prioritize well-being over consumerism. In this way, alternative lifestyles act as a form of political engagement, creating spaces for dialogue and collaboration that transcend traditional boundaries. This cultural shift fosters a deeper understanding of democracy as a dynamic process, one that thrives on creativity and authenticity.

Cultivating mindfulness within the political sphere encourages a more compassionate and engaged citizenry. As individuals become more present and aware, they develop a greater understanding of their role in the community and the interconnectedness of all lives. This heightened awareness can lead to more ethical approaches to dissent and civil disobedience, as individuals act not only out of frustration but from a place of profound consideration for the well-being of others. By recognizing the relationship between personal fulfillment and community well-being, we pave the way for a reimagined democracy—one that is resilient, responsive, and rooted in the shared human experience. Through these fresh perspectives, we can embrace the complexities of existence and channel them into meaningful social change.

ANCIENT PHILOSOPHIES AND MODERN CHANGE
Lessons from the Past

History serves as a profound teacher, illuminating the paths taken by those who dared to challenge the status quo. The struggles and triumphs of social movements throughout time reveal that the seeds of change often sprout from the fertile ground of dissent. Individuals who embraced their agency, who stood firm in their convictions, have shaped the very fabric of society. Learning from their journeys encourages us to reflect on our own roles in the ongoing quest for justice and equality. Their stories remind us that the power to enact change lies within each of us, urging us to harness our inner desires for a more fulfilling existence.

The philosophy of non-conformity emerges as a central theme in the annals of social change. Figures like Thoreau and Gandhi exemplified the strength found in civil disobedience, illustrating that true progress often requires stepping outside societal norms. Their legacies teach us that dissent is not merely an act of rebellion but a necessary catalyst for transformation. By examining their motivations and actions, we understand that non-conformity can inspire a collective awakening, fostering an environment where new ideas can flourish. In this light, we are invited to embrace our differences and recognize them as vital contributions to the democratic discourse.

Existentialism also offers valuable insights into the relationship between individual agency and political activism. The recognition of one's freedom and responsibility can ignite a passionate commitment to social justice. When we confront the absurdity of our existence and the injustices around us, we are compelled to act. The tension between personal fulfillment and societal obligation becomes a powerful motivator for change. By engaging with existentialist thought, we can find meaning in our activism, encouraging a deeper connection to our communities and the world at large. This interplay between self-actualization and collective well-being underscores the importance of nurturing both the individual spirit and the communal bond.

Alternative lifestyles, as responses to mainstream society, remind us that there are myriad ways to engage with the world. The counterculture movements of the 1960s and beyond presented radical alternatives that challenged conventional norms. These movements, rooted in the quest for authenticity, have inspired generations to rethink their relationships with consumerism, authority, and the environment. By exploring these alternative ways of living, we gain insights into the transformative power of creativity and imagination. They encourage us to redefine success and happiness, shifting our focus from material accumulation to the cultivation of relationships and experiences that enrich our lives.

The lessons from the past illuminate the path forward in reimagining democracy. By integrating unconventional philosophies with modern social movements, we can create a more inclusive and vibrant political landscape. The ethics of dissent, mindfulness in engagement, and the pursuit of happiness through justice are not only theoretical concepts but practical guides for action. As we draw inspiration from those who came before us, we are empowered to forge our own paths, creating a society that honors the complexities of humanity while striving for a more just and fulfilling existence for all.

INTEGRATING TIMELESS WISDOM IN CONTEMPORARY MOVEMENTS

Integrating timeless wisdom into contemporary movements offers a transformative lens through which we can reimagine democracy and social change. As we navigate the complexities of modern society, the teachings of ancient philosophers resonate with an urgency that invites us to reflect on our values, actions, and aspirations. The philosophies of figures such as Socrates, Confucius, and Gandhi provide not just historical insights but essential principles that can inform our approach to activism and community engagement. By grounding our movements in these enduring teachings, we cultivate a deeper understanding of our shared humanity and the moral imperatives that guide us toward a more just and equitable society.

At the heart of these timeless philosophies lies the concept of individual agency, which is essential in driving social movements. The idea that each person possesses the power to effect change is echoed in the writings of existentialists like Sartre and de Beauvoir, who emphasize personal responsibility in shaping one's destiny. By embracing this agency, individuals can become catalysts for transformation, challenging the status quo and contributing to a collective vision for a better future. This integration of personal empowerment and social responsibility encourages a vibrant interplay between individual aspirations and communal goals, fostering a sense of belonging and purpose.

Non-conformity emerges as another vital aspect of integrating ancient wisdom into modern activism. Historical figures who defied societal norms—like Thoreau with his advocacy for civil disobedience—exemplify the impact of dissent on political systems.

In a world that often prioritizes conformity over creativity, the courage to stand apart can inspire others to break free from oppressive structures. This spirit of non-conformity not only challenges existing paradigms but also invites a reevaluation of what it means to live authentically. By embracing this philosophy, activists can reclaim their narratives and invigorate movements with fresh perspectives that resonate on a personal level.

Mindfulness, rooted in ancient traditions, plays a crucial role in enhancing political engagement and promoting a philosophy of happiness intertwined with social justice. Engaging in self-reflection and cultivating awareness can help individuals remain grounded amidst the chaos of contemporary movements. This practice encourages a deeper connection to one's values and the collective vision for change, fostering resilience in the face of adversity. By prioritizing inner fulfillment, activists can inspire others to pursue not just social justice but also personal happiness, thereby creating a more harmonious society where individual well-being aligns with the greater good.

Ultimately, the integration of timeless wisdom into contemporary movements is a call to action that transcends time and culture. It invites us to reflect on our past while shaping our future, reminding us that the pursuit of a fulfilling life is intrinsically linked to the well-being of our communities. By drawing upon the teachings of those who came before us, we can forge a path that honors both individual desires and collective aspirations. In this reimagined democracy, we find strength in our shared humanity, empowering us to advocate for a world that celebrates diversity, fosters connection, and upholds justice for all.

PHILOSOPHICAL FOUNDATIONS OF DEMOCRACY

The Concept of Moral Leadership

Moral leadership stands as a beacon of hope in an era increasingly defined by authoritarianism and ethical ambiguity. In the face of oppressive regimes and systemic injustices, moral leaders emerge not merely as figures of authority but as champions of integrity, accountability, and compassion. They understand that true leadership transcends the mere wielding of power; it requires a steadfast commitment to uphold moral values, even when such principles are tested by the harsh realities of political life. This commitment invites us to reflect on what it means to lead with purpose and to inspire others to engage in the delicate dance of democracy, where every voice contributes to the collective narrative of society.

At its core, moral leadership is rooted in the understanding that personal responsibility is intertwined with democratic participation. Existentialist thought emphasizes the weight of individual choice, urging us to recognize that our actions shape the political landscape. Moral leaders embody this philosophy by not only advocating for justice but also by encouraging active engagement from those around them. They challenge us to confront the uncomfortable truths of our political systems and to take ownership of our role within them. This engagement is not passive; it requires the courage to resist complacency and to stand firm against the encroachments of dictatorship and oligarchy, reaffirming the belief that democracy thrives only when citizens are willing to fight for their rights.

Moreover, moral leadership must integrate a deep understanding of the interconnectedness of social issues, such as environmental ethics and gender equity. Eco-philosophy advocates for sustainable governance, urging leaders to recognize that the health of our planet is inextricably linked to the health of our communities. Feminist political theory further challenges traditional power structures, demanding inclusive governance that reflects the diverse tapestry of society. Moral leaders must champion these causes, dismantling oppressive systems while fostering environments where all individuals can flourish. By embracing these unconventional philosophies, they pave the way for a more just and equitable democracy.

In the digital age, the role of technology in shaping political engagement cannot be overlooked. Moral leaders must navigate the complexities of digital platforms, understanding their potential to mobilize grassroots movements while also being wary of the ways in which they can perpetuate authoritarianism. By fostering a culture of transparency and ethical discourse within these spaces, moral leadership can inspire a new generation of activists committed to social change. This engagement is crucial in reimagining democracy, as it empowers individuals to harness technology for collective action and resist the insidious effects of power that seek to silence dissent.

Ultimately, the essence of moral leadership lies in its capacity to envision and work toward a future that transcends current political challenges. It calls for a utopian ideal where justice, equity, and environmental stewardship coexist, challenging us to dream of a society that prioritizes human dignity and rights. This vision is not merely aspirational; it demands our active participation and unwavering commitment to ethical principles. As we confront the realities of authoritarianism and the abuse of power, let us embrace the call to moral leadership, recognizing that the path to true democracy is illuminated by the courage to act with integrity and compassion.

REIMAGINING DEMOCRATIC PRINCIPLES

Reimagining democratic principles involves a profound engagement with the very essence of what it means to govern and to be governed. In a world increasingly plagued by authoritarianism and oligarchic structures, the call to rethink democracy is not merely an academic exercise but a vital necessity. Embracing unconventional philosophies—whether they emerge from existentialist thought or eco-philosophy—invites us to explore new pathways that prioritize human dignity, environmental sustainability, and social justice. This reimagining is not just about political systems; it is about fostering a collective consciousness that recognizes the interconnectedness of individual agency and societal responsibility.

Existentialism offers a compelling framework for understanding personal responsibility in democratic participation. It urges individuals to confront the weight of their choices within a political landscape that often feels overwhelming and oppressive. Engaging with existentialist principles can empower citizens to reclaim their agency, motivating them to participate meaningfully in democratic processes. This active engagement is essential in countering the apathy that authoritarian systems thrive upon. When individuals recognize their role in shaping the political discourse, they can challenge the narratives that seek to diminish their rights and freedoms, thus igniting a movement toward a more participatory democracy.

In this reimagined democratic landscape, eco-philosophy plays a crucial role in integrating environmental ethics into governance. As the climate crisis looms, the principles of sustainability must be woven into the fabric of democratic ideals. This involves not only addressing environmental degradation but also ensuring that marginalized voices are included in decision-making processes. By prioritizing ecological well-being alongside social justice, we can cultivate a democracy that respects both the planet and its inhabitants. This synthesis of environmental consciousness and democratic engagement creates a resilient framework capable of addressing the multifaceted challenges of our time.

Feminist political theory further enriches the dialogue on reimagining democracy by challenging traditional power structures that have historically excluded diverse voices. By advocating for inclusive governance, feminist theories propose a model where power is decentralized and shared, allowing for a more equitable distribution of resources and opportunities. This shift not only transforms the political landscape but also fosters a culture of empathy and collaboration. As we envision a future where everyone has a seat at the table, we simultaneously dismantle patriarchal hierarchies and cultivate a democratic ethos grounded in equity and mutual respect.

Lastly, the intersection of technology and democracy presents both challenges and opportunities. Digital platforms have altered the dynamics of political engagement, enabling grassroots movements to flourish while also exposing vulnerabilities to misinformation and manipulation. To navigate this complex terrain, we must critically assess the role of technology in shaping our democratic practices. By leveraging the potential of digital tools for transparency and community-building, we can create a democratic environment that empowers citizens rather than constrains them. In this reimagined vision, democracy becomes a living, breathing entity that evolves in response to the needs and aspirations of the people, ensuring that it remains a bastion of freedom and justice in an ever-changing world.

POST-COLONIAL PERSPECTIVES ON DEMOCRACY

Historical Injustices and Their Impact

Historical injustices have left indelible marks on societies, shaping not only the political landscapes but also the moral fabric that binds communities together. The consequences of colonialism, slavery, and systemic discrimination echo through generations, fostering a pervasive sense of disenfranchisement among marginalized groups. This legacy of injustice demands a reevaluation of current political systems, urging us to confront the uncomfortable truths of our past, to ensure that the future is built on principles of equity and justice. In recognizing these historical injustices, we find the impetus for redefining democracy itself—one that is inclusive, participatory, and attentive to the voices that have historically been silenced.

As we navigate the complexities of contemporary governance, it becomes evident that the scars of the past manifest in present-day power dynamics. The authoritarian regimes that often arise from the ashes of historical oppression reveal a troubling pattern: the concentration of power in the hands of a few perpetuates cycles of inequality and injustice. The challenge, therefore, lies not only in dismantling these oppressive structures but also in fostering a political environment that embraces diverse perspectives and experiences. By integrating feminist political theory and post-colonial perspectives into our understanding of democracy, we can begin to envision a system that genuinely reflects the needs of all its constituents, particularly those who have been historically marginalized.

The existential weight of political engagement necessitates a profound sense of personal responsibility among citizens. Recognizing that each action contributes to the larger tapestry of societal change empowers individuals to become active participants in the democratic process. This engagement is not merely a right but a moral obligation, especially in the face of authoritarianism. As we cultivate a culture of accountability and participation, we create pathways for grassroots movements to thrive, challenging conventional power structures and inspiring a new vision of governance that prioritizes collective well-being over individual gain.

Moreover, the intersection of eco-philosophy and sustainable governance invites us to reconsider the very foundations of our political systems in light of environmental ethics. Historical injustices often correlate with environmental degradation, where marginalized communities bear the brunt of ecological harm. By reimagining democracy through an eco-centric lens, we can address the urgent crises of our time while simultaneously rectifying historical wrongs. This holistic approach fosters a sense of stewardship for both people and the planet, emphasizing the interconnectedness of social justice and environmental sustainability.

Ultimately, technology plays a pivotal role in shaping contemporary political engagement, presenting both challenges and opportunities. Digital platforms have the potential to amplify marginalized voices and facilitate grassroots organizing, yet they also risk entrenching existing power imbalances. To navigate this duality, we must critically assess the impact of technology on our democratic ideals, ensuring that it serves as a tool for empowerment rather than oppression. By embracing innovative approaches to governance—whether through anarchism, critical theory, or utopian visions—we can craft a future that not only addresses the injustices of the past but also paves the way for a more equitable and resilient society. In this journey, moral leadership remains paramount, guiding us toward a democratic ethos that honors the dignity and rights of all individuals.

UNCONVENTIONAL PHILOSOPHIES
Embracing Non-Traditional Ideologies

Embracing non-traditional ideologies invites individuals to explore the rich tapestry of thought that lies beyond conventional political frameworks. In a world often dominated by rigid dogmas and prescribed norms, the courage to entertain alternative philosophies can be a revolutionary act in itself. This journey towards embracing unconventional beliefs is not merely an intellectual exercise; it is a profound exploration of the self and the society we inhabit. As adults seeking a deeper understanding of our existence, we can cultivate a mindset that values diversity of thought, thereby enriching our collective experience and paving the way for transformative social change.

The role of individual agency within social movements cannot be overstated, as it is the unique contributions of each person that ignite broader transformations.

By embracing non-traditional ideologies, individuals unlock their potential to challenge oppressive systems and envision new possibilities. This agency is amplified when individuals recognize their inner desires for fulfillment and authenticity. It is here that we find the intersection of personal growth and political activism, where the act of dissent becomes a powerful expression of one's identity and beliefs. Each act of defiance against societal norms serves as a reminder that change begins within, emanating outward to inspire others.

Non-conformity has historically played a pivotal role in shaping political systems. Those who dare to think differently challenge existing power structures, often at great personal cost, yet their contributions are invaluable. By questioning the status quo and standing firm in their convictions, non-conformists disrupt complacency and provoke essential dialogues about justice, equality, and freedom. This disruption is not merely chaos; it is a necessary catalyst for evolution, prompting society to reevaluate its values and priorities. As we embrace these non-traditional ideologies, we become part of a larger narrative that honors dissent as a vital thread in the fabric of democracy.

The intersection of existentialism and political activism offers rich philosophical ground for those seeking to live more authentically in a society that often feels alienating. Existentialist thought emphasizes individual meaning-making and personal responsibility, urging us to confront the absurdities of existence. When we apply these principles to political engagement, we recognize that our actions are driven by a desire for authenticity and social justice. Embracing this ideological framework not only empowers us as individuals but also aligns our personal aspirations with a collective vision for a just and equitable society. We learn that our struggles for meaning mirror the broader fight for social change, reinforcing the interconnectedness of our journeys.

Ultimately, the pursuit of alternative lifestyles in response to mainstream society embodies a profound commitment to living in alignment with our values. By rejecting the pressures of conformity, we carve out spaces for creativity, compassion, and community well-being.

This lifestyle choice is not merely a rejection of societal norms; it is an affirmation of our belief in a more humane and just world. As we embrace non-traditional ideologies, we cultivate a philosophy of happiness that intertwines personal fulfillment with social responsibility. In doing so, we not only enrich our own lives but also contribute to the flourishing of our communities, fostering an environment where diverse ideas can thrive and democracy can be reimagined in ways that honor the complexity of the human experience.

THE POWER OF DIVERGENT THINKING

Divergent thinking serves as a powerful catalyst for reimagining democracy and addressing the complex challenges of our time. It invites individuals to step outside the confines of conventional thought and embrace a multitude of perspectives, fostering creativity and innovation in political discourse and social movements. In a world that often seems rigid and predetermined, the ability to think divergently empowers people to envision alternative pathways toward social justice and community well-being. It encourages us to explore not just what is, but what could be, igniting a spark of hope and possibility within us.

At its core, divergent thinking nurtures the inner desire for a more fulfilling life, urging individuals to reject the status quo that often stifles genuine expression and personal growth. This mindset aligns with the philosophies of existentialism, which emphasize individual agency and the importance of making authentic choices in the face of societal pressures. By embracing unconventional thinking, we can break free from the limitations imposed by mainstream ideologies and cultivate a more profound understanding of our values and aspirations. This journey toward self-discovery is not merely personal; it has the potential to inspire collective action and transformative change.

The impact of non-conformity on political systems cannot be underestimated. Those who dare to think differently often become the pioneers of change, challenging entrenched norms and inspiring others to question the legitimacy of oppressive structures. History is replete with examples of social movements that have thrived on divergent thinking, as individuals united by a shared vision of justice and equity mobilize to dismantle barriers that hinder progress. By fostering a culture that celebrates non-conformity, we can create an environment where innovative ideas flourish, leading to the emergence of new paradigms in governance and civic engagement.

As we navigate the intersection of alternative lifestyles and mainstream society, it becomes evident that the choices we make as individuals can have profound implications for the collective. Embracing diverse ways of living can serve as a form of resistance against a homogenizing culture that often prioritizes conformity over creativity. This rebellion against the mundane not only enhances personal fulfillment but also strengthens community bonds, as individuals come together to support one another in their quests for meaning and joy. In this way, divergent thinking becomes a collective endeavor, enriching the fabric of society and fostering resilience in the face of adversity.

Ultimately, the philosophy of happiness in the context of social justice hinges on our ability to dream beyond the limitations of conventional thought. Mindfulness and awareness of our thoughts and choices empower us to engage thoughtfully with the world around us. By cultivating an attitude of curiosity and openness, we can explore the ethical dimensions of dissent and civil disobedience, understanding that such actions arise from a deep-seated desire for a more equitable society. This alignment of personal fulfillment with community well-being is the essence of reimagining democracy—an invitation to embrace the power of divergent thinking as we strive for a world that honors both individuality and collective purpose.

TECHNOLOGY AND DEMOCRACY

The Influence of Digital Platforms

The rise of digital platforms has profoundly reshaped the landscape of political engagement, presenting both unprecedented opportunities and significant challenges. In an era where information flows freely, these platforms have become vital tools for organizing, mobilizing, and expressing dissent against authoritarian regimes. They empower individuals to share their narratives, fostering a sense of community that transcends geographical boundaries. The democratization of information through social media and online forums enables marginalized voices to be heard, challenging traditional power structures and inspiring collective action. Yet, this newfound agency comes with the responsibility of navigating a complex digital environment rife with misinformation and manipulation, necessitating a critical examination of the ethics surrounding these platforms.

As we explore the influence of digital platforms on political dynamics, it becomes essential to recognize their dual capacity for liberation and oppression. While they can amplify democratic ideals, they also serve as instruments of surveillance and control.

Governments and corporations often exploit these technologies to monitor dissent and suppress free expression. This paradox calls for a philosophical inquiry into the nature of power in the digital age. How can we cultivate a political engagement that not only utilizes these platforms for social change but also safeguards the rights and freedoms of individuals? Embracing a critical perspective allows us to challenge the exploitative uses of technology while promoting ethical frameworks that prioritize human dignity and autonomy.

Digital platforms also facilitate new forms of grassroots activism, embodying the principles of anarchism and alternative governance. They provide spaces for non-hierarchical organization, enabling communities to engage in direct action and participatory decision-making. This shift towards decentralized models of governance offers a refreshing departure from traditional political structures that often perpetuate inequality. Empowered by digital tools, individuals can forge connections, share resources, and coordinate efforts that challenge the status quo. Such movements highlight the potential for a more inclusive and equitable democracy, one that resonates with the ideals of feminist political theory and post-colonial perspectives, acknowledging the historical injustices that continue to shape our political realities.

In reimagining democracy through the lens of eco-philosophy, digital platforms play a crucial role in raising awareness about environmental issues and fostering sustainable governance. The interconnectedness facilitated by these technologies allows for the dissemination of information on ecological crises, galvanizing collective action rooted in environmental ethics. By harnessing the power of digital platforms, activists can advocate for policies that prioritize the planet and its inhabitants, aligning political engagement with existential responsibilities. This synergy between technology and sustainability underscores the importance of integrating ethical considerations into our political frameworks, ensuring that our pursuit of progress does not come at the expense of our shared future.

Ultimately, the influence of digital platforms invites us to reflect on our moral responsibilities as citizens in a rapidly evolving political landscape. It challenges us to engage critically with the tools at our disposal, fostering a culture of responsible participation that resists authoritarianism and promotes human rights. By embracing unconventional philosophies and prioritizing ethical leadership, we can harness the transformative potential of digital platforms to reimagine democratic practice. In doing so, we not only confront the pressing challenges of our time but also cultivate a robust moral framework that champions justice, inclusivity, and the intrinsic value of every individual within the tapestry of our global society.

POWER DYNAMICS IN THE AGE OF INFORMATION

In the Age of Information, power dynamics have dramatically transformed, challenging traditional notions of authority and governance. The rise of digital platforms has democratized access to information, empowering individuals to engage in political discourse like never before. Yet, this newfound power is a double-edged sword; while it enables grassroots movements and amplifies marginalized voices, it also opens avenues for manipulation and surveillance. In this context, the ethical responsibility of leaders becomes paramount, as they navigate the complexities of technological advancements while upholding democratic values and human rights.

Philosophical perspectives on power dynamics reveal the intricate relationship between technology and democracy. The traditional hierarchies of political authority are increasingly undermined by the decentralized nature of digital platforms, which can facilitate both collective action and authoritarian control. Individuals are called to embrace their existential responsibility, recognizing that political engagement is not merely a right but an ethical imperative. As we confront the dangers of oligarchic systems and the erosion of civil liberties, the challenge lies in reimagining governance through a lens that prioritizes inclusivity and participatory practices.

Eco-philosophy introduces an essential dimension to our understanding of power in contemporary society. The intersection of environmental ethics and governance underscores the urgent need for sustainable practices that transcend traditional political boundaries. By prioritizing ecological well-being, we can reframe democracy to reflect a holistic understanding of human rights that includes the rights of the planet itself. This rethinking compels us to confront the existential threats posed by climate change and environmental degradation, urging individuals and leaders alike to adopt a moral stance that prioritizes long-term sustainability over short-term gains.

Feminist political theory further enriches the discourse on power dynamics, challenging entrenched structures that perpetuate inequality. By advocating for inclusive governance, feminist perspectives illuminate the ways in which traditional power dynamics often exclude diverse voices. This call for equity is not merely a plea for representation; it is a fundamental reconfiguration of how we understand authority. As we seek to dismantle oppressive systems, the integration of feminist insights into political philosophy can inspire innovative approaches to leadership that embrace collaboration and intersectionality.

Finally, the exploration of post-colonial perspectives on democracy invites us to reckon with historical injustices that continue to shape our political landscape. Recognizing the enduring impacts of colonialism allows for a deeper understanding of current power dynamics and the necessity for reparative justice. In this reimagined framework, democracy becomes a vehicle for healing and transformation, urging societies to confront their past while envisioning a future that honors the rights and dignities of all individuals. The collective engagement in these philosophical explorations equips us to stand firm against authoritarianism, fostering a resilient and compassionate approach to governance that champions both human rights and ethical leadership.

ENGAGING CITIZENS THROUGH TECHNOLOGY

Engaging citizens through technology has emerged as a pivotal aspect of revitalizing democratic practices in an era marked by authoritarianism and oligarchic tendencies. Digital platforms provide unprecedented opportunities for participation, allowing individuals to voice their opinions, mobilize movements, and hold power to account. By harnessing technology, we can create a more inclusive political landscape that empowers citizens to reclaim their agency. The challenge lies not only in the development of these tools but also in fostering a culture of ethical engagement that prioritizes transparency, accountability, and active participation.

As we navigate the complexities of modern governance, it is essential to recognize the role of technology as a double-edged sword. While it can facilitate democratic engagement, it also poses risks of surveillance and manipulation. The ethical considerations surrounding data privacy and the potential for misinformation must be at the forefront of our discussions. By promoting digital literacy and critical thinking, we can equip citizens with the tools they need to discern truth from falsehood and to engage meaningfully with the information that shapes their lives. This approach encourages a collective responsibility toward sustaining a vibrant democratic discourse.

Moreover, engaging citizens through technology creates avenues for marginalized voices to be heard, challenging traditional power structures that often exclude them. Feminist political theory emphasizes the importance of inclusivity in governance, and technology can serve as a platform for diverse perspectives. Collaborative platforms can amplify the narratives of those historically silenced, fostering a more equitable political environment. By embracing these unconventional philosophies, we can reimagine democracy as a space that values every individual's contribution, thereby enriching the collective decision-making process.

In an age where environmental crises demand urgent attention, eco-philosophy and sustainable governance must also intersect with our technological endeavors. We can leverage digital tools to promote environmental awareness and action, connecting citizens to local and global ecological movements. Engaging in eco-centric governance through technology not only fosters a sense of shared responsibility but also cultivates a commitment to sustainability that transcends political boundaries. This holistic approach to democratic engagement encourages citizens to consider the interconnectedness of social justice and environmental stewardship.

Ultimately, the engagement of citizens through technology is a testament to our collective moral responsibility in shaping the future of democracy. Existentialist thought urges individuals to embrace their agency, recognizing that political participation is not just a right but a duty. By fostering a culture of active engagement and ethical leadership, we can stand firmly against authoritarianism and envision a more just and equitable society.

The philosophical underpinnings of our actions, informed by critical theory and post-colonial perspectives, will guide us in creating a political landscape that honors human rights and embodies the values of inclusivity, transparency, and sustainability.

ETHICS AND AUTHORITY
MORAL LEADERSHIP IN THE FACE OF AUTHORITARIANISM

The Crisis of Authority
Understanding Authoritarianism

Understanding authoritarianism requires a deep dive into the nature of power and the mechanisms by which it is wielded. At its core, authoritarianism thrives on the suppression of dissent and the concentration of power in the hands of a few. This system distorts the very essence of democracy, which is built upon the principle of participation and the protection of individual rights. As we navigate the complexities of contemporary politics, it becomes crucial to dissect the elements that allow authoritarian regimes to flourish and to recognize the subtle encroachments on freedoms that can lead to a broader acceptance of such systems.

Philosophically, the challenge lies in understanding our responsibilities as citizens within a democratic framework. Existentialism offers a lens through which we can examine our personal engagement in political processes. Each individual bears the weight of their choices and actions, and in a democratic society, this translates into a duty to resist authoritarianism. Embracing the notion that our voices matter, we must cultivate a culture of active participation, ensuring that our moral compass guides us in standing against oppression and advocating for a more just society.

In considering alternative forms of governance, eco-philosophy invites us to rethink democracy through the prism of environmental ethics. The intersection of ecological sustainability and political engagement presents a compelling argument for redefining power structures. By prioritizing the well-being of our planet and its inhabitants, we challenge the short-sightedness often associated with authoritarian regimes that exploit natural resources for immediate gain. This approach calls for a governance model that is both inclusive and sustainable, emphasizing the interconnectedness of social justice and environmental stewardship.

Feminist political theory further enriches our understanding of authoritarianism by challenging traditional power hierarchies. It highlights the necessity of inclusive governance that reflects diverse voices and experiences. By dismantling patriarchal structures, we can envision a political landscape that empowers all individuals, fostering resilience against the allure of authoritarian rule. This reimagining of power dynamics is essential in creating a society where every person has the opportunity to influence decision-making processes, thereby reinforcing democratic ideals.

Lastly, the advent of technology has transformed political engagement, presenting both opportunities and challenges. Digital platforms can amplify voices and mobilize movements, but they can also exacerbate divisions and facilitate the spread of misinformation. To combat authoritarianism, it is imperative to cultivate a critical understanding of these technologies and their impact on our democratic processes. By harnessing the potential of digital tools for social change, we can foster a more participatory and informed citizenry, ultimately paving the way for a future where ethical leadership prevails and authoritarianism is met with unwavering resistance.

THE EROSION OF TRUST IN LEADERSHIP

The erosion of trust in leadership is a profound challenge that has emerged in contemporary society, reflecting a broader crisis of faith in institutions and those who govern. As citizens, we find ourselves grappling with a landscape marked by betrayal, corruption, and the relentless encroachment of authoritarianism. This decay of trust is not merely a political issue; it is an existential one that calls for a reevaluation of our relationship with authority and a commitment to reimagining democracy. It compels us to question how we can cultivate a system of governance that aligns more closely with our ethical values and aspirations for a just society.

In the face of rising authoritarian regimes and the entrenchment of oligarchic structures, the failure of leadership to uphold moral principles has led to disillusionment and disengagement among the populace. This disillusionment reveals a critical need for ethical leadership that embraces transparency, accountability, and inclusivity. As we confront the dangerous path of limited rights and abuses of power, we must draw upon diverse philosophical perspectives to forge a new understanding of democratic engagement—one that actively challenges traditional hierarchies and envisions a more equitable distribution of power. The voices of marginalized communities, particularly those informed by feminist political theory and post-colonial perspectives, must be amplified in this discourse to dismantle the oppressive structures that have long dominated our political landscapes.

Moreover, the intersection of technology and democracy offers both opportunities and challenges in rebuilding trust within our leadership. Digital platforms have the potential to democratize information and empower grassroots movements, yet they also pose risks of manipulation and misinformation. As we navigate this digital age, we must critically engage with the tools at our disposal, ensuring they serve to enhance participatory governance rather than undermine it. By fostering a culture of ethical digital engagement, we can reclaim agency in our political lives and reestablish trust in the systems designed to represent our collective interests.

The role of ethics in political leadership cannot be overstated. It requires leaders to embody moral responsibility, particularly in combating the resurgence of authoritarianism. Ethical leadership demands a commitment to human rights and a recognition of the intrinsic value of every individual within the political framework. By prioritizing ethical considerations, we can inspire a new generation of leaders who are not only willing to challenge the status quo but are also equipped to envision a more just and sustainable future. This vision must be grounded in eco-philosophy, recognizing that our environmental responsibilities are intertwined with our social and political obligations.

Ultimately, the erosion of trust in leadership offers us an opportunity for profound transformation. It invites us to reimagine democratic participation through the lens of existentialism, recognizing our personal responsibility in shaping the governance structures that govern our lives. By embracing unconventional philosophies and fostering a culture of critical engagement, we can challenge the prevailing paradigms that perpetuate injustice. In doing so, we pave the way for a future where leadership is not merely a reflection of authority but a manifestation of our shared ethical commitments, enabling us to stand firm against tyranny and work towards a more just and inclusive society.

HISTORICAL CONTEXT OF POWER ABUSE

Throughout history, the abuse of power has manifested in various forms, intertwining with the fabric of human civilization and shaping societies in profound ways. From ancient empires wielding absolute authority over their subjects to contemporary regimes that employ sophisticated mechanisms of control, the historical context of power abuse reveals a persistent struggle between authority and individual rights. This struggle highlights the consequences of unchecked power, as well as the moral imperative for leaders to embrace ethical governance. As we examine these past examples, we find that they serve not only as cautionary tales but also as catalysts for reimagining democratic principles that prioritize the dignity and autonomy of every individual.

The philosophical underpinnings of power abuse often reveal deep-seated societal issues that transcend time and geography. In many instances, the concentration of power has led to the marginalization of entire groups, echoing the themes found in feminist political theory and post-colonial perspectives. These frameworks challenge conventional power structures, advocating for inclusivity and the recognition of historical injustices. By understanding how power has been wielded to oppress and exploit, we can begin to dismantle the barriers that have perpetuated inequality and envision a more equitable future. This requires acknowledging the historical context of domination while simultaneously embracing new, unconventional philosophies that prioritize social change and collective well-being.

Existentialism offers a compelling lens through which to view personal responsibility in democratic participation. Each individual is called to reflect on their role within the political landscape, recognizing that passive acceptance of authority can lead to complicity in systems of oppression. This notion of active engagement is essential in confronting authoritarianism and oligarchic structures that threaten the rights of humanity. By fostering a culture of accountability, individuals can reclaim their agency, advocating for governance that is rooted in ethical principles and respect for human rights. The path to meaningful democracy is paved with the recognition that each voice matters, and that collective action can challenge the status quo.

In the face of environmental crises, eco-philosophy introduces a vital dimension to our understanding of governance and democracy. The abuse of power often aligns with exploitative practices that disregard ecological integrity and the well-being of future generations. By rethinking democracy through environmental ethics, we can forge new alliances that prioritize sustainability and justice. This perspective compels us to critique not only the political systems that facilitate ecological harm but also our own roles as citizens within these frameworks. Embracing sustainable governance is not merely an ethical stance; it is a necessary evolution in our quest for a just society that honors both human rights and the planet.

Technology, while a powerful tool for democratization, can also exacerbate existing power imbalances. The digital age has transformed political engagement, presenting both opportunities and challenges in the fight against authoritarianism. As we analyze the impact of digital platforms on power dynamics, we must remain vigilant about their potential for manipulation and control. Critical theory and social change provide valuable insights into how culture and ideology shape our political realities, urging us to interrogate the narratives that dominate public discourse. By envisioning utopian and dystopian futures, we can better understand the implications of our choices today. Ultimately, the historical context of power abuse serves as a reminder of our moral responsibilities in political leadership, urging us to stand firm against tyranny and advocate for a democratic vision that is inclusive, sustainable, and just.

RESPONDING TO CURRENT POLITICAL CHALLENGES

In the face of current political challenges, responding with a blend of ethical reflection and active engagement becomes imperative. As we navigate a landscape marked by rising authoritarianism, oligarchic tendencies, and the erosion of fundamental human rights, it is crucial to reimagine the essence of democracy. This requires us to embrace unconventional philosophies that advocate for social change and personal transformation. By grounding our actions in a deep understanding of existential responsibility, we can cultivate a political engagement that resonates with the core tenets of our humanity, empowering individuals to resist oppressive systems and envision a more just society.

Feminist political theory urges us to challenge traditional power structures that have long dictated the terms of governance. By amplifying the voices of marginalized groups, we can foster an inclusive political environment that recognizes the diverse experiences and needs of all citizens. This shift not only enriches democratic discourse but also enhances our collective capacity to confront the injustices perpetuated by authoritarian regimes. In this light, ethical leadership becomes a vehicle for promoting equity and dismantling the barriers that hinder meaningful participation in the democratic process.

From a post-colonial perspective, we are called to reimagine political systems through the lens of historical injustices. Acknowledging the legacies of colonialism and their enduring impact on contemporary governance allows us to confront the systemic inequalities that persist today. By integrating these insights into our political engagement, we can challenge the status quo and advocate for a more equitable distribution of power. This requires not only a critical examination of existing structures but also the courage to envision alternative forms of governance that prioritize justice and sustainability.

The intersection of technology and democracy presents both challenges and opportunities for political engagement. As digital platforms reshape the dynamics of power and participation, it is essential to critically analyze their role in facilitating or hindering democratic processes. By harnessing technology as a tool for empowerment, we can create new spaces for dialogue and activism that transcend traditional boundaries. This necessitates a commitment to ethical practices in the digital realm, ensuring that our engagement is grounded in principles that uphold human dignity and collective well-being.

Ultimately, the journey toward a more just and sustainable democracy requires a synthesis of various philosophical perspectives, from eco-philosophy to anarchism. By exploring grassroots movements and non-hierarchical systems, we can cultivate a political culture that prioritizes collaboration and mutual support. In doing so, we not only envision utopian futures but also recognize the importance of confronting dystopian realities. Embracing our moral responsibilities as citizens, we can stand firm against the forces that threaten our rights and freedoms, forging a path toward a more inclusive and ethical governance for all.

COMBATING AUTHORITARIAN REGIMES THROUGH ETHICS

In the heart of every society lies a complex interplay between authority and ethics, a dance that often determines the fate of democratic values and human rights. Combating authoritarian regimes requires not only a rejection of oppressive systems but also a profound commitment to ethical principles that uplift the human spirit. This moral dedication acts as a beacon, guiding individuals and communities toward a vision of governance that respects dignity and promotes justice. By fostering an ethical framework that prioritizes human rights, we can challenge the very foundations of authoritarianism, bringing forth a renaissance of democratic engagement and responsibility.

Ethics must serve as our compass in the turbulent waters of political engagement, especially in the face of dictatorship and oligarchy. As we navigate these challenges, we must embrace existentialist principles that emphasize personal responsibility in democratic participation. Every individual holds the power to influence the course of society, and recognizing this power is essential. By actively participating in political processes and advocating for ethical governance, we can dismantle the narratives that empower authoritarian regimes. Each act of resistance, no matter how small, contributes to a collective voice that demands accountability and justice.

Moreover, the intersection of eco-philosophy and sustainable governance presents a unique opportunity to reimagine democracy through an ethical lens. In an era marked by environmental crises, addressing the ecological implications of governance is crucial. Authoritarian regimes often exploit natural resources without regard for future generations, perpetuating cycles of oppression and environmental degradation. By advocating for policies rooted in environmental ethics, we can challenge these destructive practices and promote a more inclusive and sustainable democratic model. This approach not only addresses ecological concerns but also affirms the interconnectedness of human rights and environmental justice.

Feminist political theory further enriches our understanding of ethics in combating authoritarianism by challenging traditional power structures. By embracing inclusive governance that values diverse voices, we dismantle the patriarchal systems that often support authoritarian rule. This ethical commitment to equality and representation not only empowers marginalized groups but also strengthens the democratic fabric of society. When every individual has a stake in governance, the potential for systemic change grows, fostering a political landscape where justice and equity prevail.

Finally, as we stand firm against the rising tide of authoritarianism, we must also critically examine the influence of technology on democratic engagement. Digital platforms can serve as powerful tools for mobilization, yet they also harbor the potential for manipulation and control. By understanding the complexities of technology in shaping power dynamics, we can harness its potential for ethical political engagement. This awareness equips us to confront the challenges posed by authoritarian regimes, ensuring that our pursuit of democracy remains rooted in ethical principles that champion human rights, social justice, and sustainable governance. In this endeavor, we are not mere spectators; we are active participants in shaping a future that honors the intrinsic value of every individual and the collective strength of our shared humanity.

OLIGARCHY AND TYRANNY
Defining Oligarchy

Oligarchy, a term derived from the Greek words "oligos" meaning few and "arkho" meaning to rule, refers to a political system in which power is concentrated in the hands of a small group of individuals or families. This concentration often leads to a governance structure that prioritizes the interests of the few over the needs of the many. Understanding the intricacies of oligarchy is essential for grasping how power dynamics shape societies, influence economic inequality, and impact the very fabric of human rights. In a world increasingly dominated by a handful of powerful entities, recognizing the characteristics and implications of oligarchic rule is vital for fostering a society that values equity and justice.

The influence of oligarchies on economic inequality cannot be overstated. In such systems, wealth and resources are often hoarded by the elite, creating a chasm between the privileged few and the marginalized many. This imbalance not only stifles economic mobility but also fosters an environment where social justice remains elusive. By examining the mechanisms through which oligarchies operate, we can better understand how they perpetuate cycles of poverty and disenfranchisement. Engaging in discussions about the ramifications of this concentration of power is crucial for initiating change and advocating for more equitable economic policies that prioritize the welfare of all citizens.

Human rights advocacy becomes particularly challenging in oligarchic regimes. The very structure of these governments often leads to the suppression of dissent, limiting the freedoms of expression, assembly, and association. In such environments, those who dare to challenge the status quo or advocate for the rights of the marginalized face significant risks. Yet, history has shown that resilience can emerge from oppression. By studying the tactics of grassroots movements and the strategies employed by human rights defenders, individuals can gain valuable insights into how to navigate and resist the constraints imposed by oligarchies, fostering a culture of advocacy even in the most repressive circumstances.

Political education and civic engagement are paramount in empowering the youth to challenge oligarchic structures. By equipping young individuals with knowledge about their rights, the political process, and the importance of participation, societies can cultivate a generation that is not only aware of the dynamics at play but also equipped to instigate change. Engaging youth in discussions about the relationship between political systems and social justice can inspire them to become advocates for their communities, ensuring that the voices of the marginalized are amplified and that the principles of democracy are upheld.

Lastly, the role of international organizations in promoting human rights cannot be underestimated in the context of oligarchy. These entities often serve as watchdogs, holding governments accountable for their actions and advocating for the rights of individuals worldwide. By fostering partnerships with local organizations and supporting grassroots movements, international bodies can help create a network of advocacy that transcends borders. This collaborative effort is vital for challenging the hegemony of oligarchic systems and promoting a global culture of respect for human rights, thereby laying the groundwork for societies that thrive in times of adversity.

THE NATURE OF TYRANNY

The nature of tyranny is a complex tapestry woven from threads of power, oppression, and the human spirit's indomitable quest for freedom. Tyranny emerges when authority becomes concentrated in the hands of a few, often at the expense of the many. This concentration leads to a systematic erosion of human rights and civil liberties, as those in power prioritize their interests over the welfare of the populace. Understanding the mechanisms of tyranny is essential for recognizing its symptoms in contemporary society. It compels us to reflect on our own political systems and the importance of vigilance in safeguarding democracy against the encroachments of authoritarianism.

Tyranny manifests in various forms, from overt oppression to subtler mechanisms of control that stifle dissent and manipulate public perception. The oligarchic structures that underlie many modern political systems often serve to perpetuate inequality and disenfranchisement. In such environments, economic power translates into political power, creating a vicious cycle that marginalizes voices advocating for social justice. Recognizing the relationship between economic disparity and political tyranny is crucial. When wealth is concentrated, the potential for abuse of power grows, leading to a society where the few dictate the lives of the many, ultimately threatening the fundamental principles of democracy and equality.

In historical contexts, tyranny has often been met with resistance, illustrating the resilience of the human spirit. Case studies of tyrannical regimes reveal patterns of dissent and the emergence of civil society movements that challenge oppressive structures. These narratives serve as powerful reminders that the struggle against tyranny is not only a fight for rights but also a testament to the strength of collective action. Engaging with these histories equips individuals with the knowledge to recognize the signs of tyranny in their own lives and empowers them to take a stand against injustice, fostering a culture of civic engagement and political awareness.

The role of international organizations in promoting human rights cannot be overstated, particularly in authoritarian regimes where local advocacy may be suppressed. These organizations serve as beacons of hope, amplifying the voices of those silenced by tyranny and holding oppressive governments accountable. They provide a framework for global solidarity, urging nations to uphold human rights standards and supporting grassroots movements that seek to reclaim agency. In times of adversity, the collaboration between local advocates and international bodies becomes a critical lifeline for those suffering under authoritarian rule, reminding us that the quest for freedom transcends borders.

Fostering a healthy society requires a commitment to understanding the dynamics of power and the importance of political education. It is essential for youth to engage with the concepts of tyranny and oligarchy, as well as the mechanisms of resistance, to cultivate informed citizens ready to challenge injustice. By instilling a robust sense of civic responsibility, we can inspire the next generation to advocate for human rights and social justice, ensuring that the lessons of the past inform the actions of the future. In doing so, we not only confront the nature of tyranny but also illuminate the path toward a more equitable and just society, resilient in the face of adversity.

THE IMPACT OF OLIGARCHIES ON SOCIETY

The impact of oligarchies on society is profound and multifaceted, shaping the very fabric of political, economic, and social life. At their core, oligarchies concentrate power in the hands of a few, often leading to a system where wealth and influence dictate the rules of engagement. This concentration can result in significant economic inequality, where resources and opportunities are hoarded by a privileged elite. Such disparities foster a society where the majority feels disenfranchised, leading to social unrest and a pervasive sense of injustice. Understanding this dynamic is essential for those who wish to advocate for a more equitable distribution of power and resources.

Economic inequality in oligarchic systems often stifles social mobility and creates barriers to opportunity. The oligarchs, by wielding disproportionate influence over political systems, can manipulate policies to protect their interests, leaving the lower and middle classes struggling to survive. This creates a vicious cycle—economic power begets political power, which in turn perpetuates economic disparities. As wealth becomes increasingly concentrated, the gap between the affluent and the impoverished widens, eroding the social contract and creating conditions ripe for conflict. Recognizing the signs of such inequality is critical for citizens and advocates alike, as it empowers them to challenge the status quo and demand systemic change.

Human rights advocacy often faces significant hurdles in authoritarian regimes characterized by oligarchic rule. The concentration of power in the hands of a few typically leads to the suppression of dissent and the marginalization of voices advocating for justice and equality. In these environments, the fight for human rights becomes an act of courage, as individuals and organizations risk persecution to uphold fundamental freedoms. By shining a light on these struggles, we not only honor the resilience of those fighting for their rights but also inspire a broader movement for social justice that transcends national borders. The global community must remain vigilant and supportive, recognizing that the fight for human rights is intertwined with the struggle against oligarchic oppression.

Political education and civic engagement are essential tools for youth in combating the challenges posed by oligarchies. By fostering a culture of critical thinking and active participation, young people can challenge entrenched power structures and advocate for policies that promote equity and justice. Empowering the next generation to understand the intricacies of political systems equips them with the knowledge necessary to engage effectively in civic life. This engagement can take many forms, from grassroots organizing to digital activism, but the underlying principle remains the same: an informed and active citizenry is a bulwark against the tyranny of the few.

The role of international organizations in promoting human rights cannot be overstated, especially in contexts dominated by oligarchic rule. These entities serve as watchdogs, providing platforms for advocacy and amplifying the voices of those marginalized by oppressive regimes. By facilitating dialogue, offering resources, and applying diplomatic pressure, international organizations can help to dismantle the structures that uphold oligarchies and foster environments where human rights are respected and upheld. The comparative analysis of oligarchies and democracies reveals that while the former often leads to oppression and inequality, the latter can cultivate societies that thrive on justice and inclusion. As we strive for a more just world, understanding the impact of oligarchies becomes not just an academic exercise, but a call to action for all who believe in the power of democracy to uplift society.

ECONOMIC INEQUALITY AND OLIGARCHIC STRUCTURES
The Link Between Oligarchy and Economic Disparities

The relationship between oligarchy and economic disparities is a critical lens through which we can examine the mechanisms of power that shape our societies. Oligarchies, characterized by the concentration of power in the hands of a few, often lead to profound economic inequalities. In such systems, wealth is not only accumulated but also preserved within a select group, resulting in a stark divide between the affluent elite and the broader population. This disparity is not merely an economic issue; it reflects a deeper systemic imbalance that undermines the principles of equity and justice. Understanding this link is vital for fostering a society that values human rights and strives for genuine democratic engagement.

In oligarchic structures, the privileged few wield significant influence over policy decisions, often prioritizing their interests over the common good. This concentration of power manifests in various ways, including tax policies that favor the wealthy, regulatory frameworks that protect corporate monopolies, and public services that become increasingly inaccessible to the lower and middle classes. As a result, economic mobility diminishes, and the gap between the rich and poor widens. The impact of such inequalities extends beyond mere financial metrics; it stifles social cohesion and diminishes trust in institutions, leading to a populace that feels disenfranchised and voiceless.

Moreover, the repercussions of oligarchic governance are particularly pronounced in times of adversity. Economic downturns, natural disasters, or public health crises often exacerbate existing disparities, as those with wealth and resources can insulate themselves from the worst effects. In contrast, marginalized communities bear the brunt of these challenges, facing increased hardships without adequate support from a government that prioritizes the interests of the elite. This reality calls for a renewed commitment to human rights advocacy, emphasizing the need for systems that uplift all citizens rather than perpetuating cycles of inequality.

Education and civic engagement play crucial roles in challenging the status quo of oligarchies and their economic ramifications. By fostering political awareness among youth and encouraging active participation in democratic processes, societies can build a foundation for resilience against oligarchic manipulation. Empowering individuals with knowledge about their rights and the importance of equitable policies cultivates a generation that values justice and equity. This engagement is not merely an idealistic pursuit; it is an essential strategy for dismantling the structures that sustain economic disparities.

International organizations also hold significant potential in addressing the link between oligarchy and economic inequality. Through advocacy, monitoring, and support for grassroots movements, these entities can help promote human rights and equitable economic policies. Comparative analyses of oligarchies and democracies reveal that systems promoting accountability and transparency tend to yield more equitable outcomes. As we navigate the complexities of power dynamics, it is imperative to recognize the interconnectedness of political systems, economic justice, and human rights. By doing so, we can inspire collective action that champions a more just and equitable society for all.

CASE STUDIES OF ECONOMIC INEQUALITY

In the landscape of economic inequality, case studies serve as powerful illustrations of how political systems shape the distribution of wealth and opportunity within societies. One notable example is the stark disparity witnessed in post-Soviet Russia, where the transition from a planned economy to a market-driven one created a new class of oligarchs. This group, comprising a few individuals with close ties to political power, amassed vast fortunes while the majority of the population faced economic hardships. By analyzing this case, we can observe how the intertwining of political influence and economic gain leads to systemic inequality, reinforcing the importance of vigilance against the dangers of oligarchy that can stifle social mobility and justice.

Another compelling case study can be found in the context of Venezuela, where the government's shift toward authoritarian rule has exacerbated economic disparities. The concentration of power in the hands of a small elite, coupled with mismanagement of resources, has resulted in one of the worst economic crises in modern history. The impact on human rights has been severe, with citizens facing food shortages, hyperinflation, and political repression. This situation underscores the critical need for human rights advocacy, highlighting how tyranny can entrench economic inequality and diminish the prospects for a thriving society. The resilience of the Venezuelan people, however, showcases the power of civic engagement and the unyielding pursuit of justice, even in the face of overwhelming adversity.

Examining the case of South Africa post-apartheid reveals the complexities of addressing historical inequalities within a democratic framework. While the nation has made significant strides in establishing a political system that promotes equality, economic disparities remain pervasive. The legacy of apartheid continues to influence wealth distribution, raising questions about the effectiveness of policies aimed at redressing past injustices. This example illustrates the vital relationship between political systems and social justice, emphasizing that democracy alone is insufficient without active efforts to dismantle systemic barriers to equity. Engaging youth in political education becomes essential, as their involvement is crucial for sustaining the momentum toward a more equitable society.

The role of international organizations, such as the United Nations, in promoting human rights and addressing economic inequality also merits examination. These entities often serve as beacons of hope, advocating for policies that aim to reduce disparities and promote social justice on a global scale. For instance, initiatives focused on sustainable development and poverty alleviation reflect a recognition of the interconnectedness of economic systems and human rights. By fostering collaboration among nations, international organizations can amplify the voices of marginalized groups, challenging the status quo and pushing for reforms that benefit society as a whole.

Lastly, a comparative analysis of oligarchies and democracies reveals critical insights into the mechanisms that perpetuate economic inequality. Countries like Brazil, where political corruption has allowed for the concentration of wealth and power, stand in stark contrast to more equitable democracies that prioritize transparency and accountability. Understanding these dynamics not only illuminates the challenges faced by various societies but also inspires action toward reform. Each case study serves as a reminder that while the struggle against economic inequality is complex and multifaceted, the collective efforts of informed citizens and resilient communities can pave the way for a future where social justice thrives, even amidst adversity.

SOLUTIONS FOR ECONOMIC JUSTICE

Economic justice is a fundamental pillar in the quest for a fair and equitable society, especially in the face of pervasive inequality exacerbated by oligarchic structures. To address this, we must advocate for policies that promote wealth redistribution through progressive taxation, social welfare programs, and equitable access to education and healthcare. These initiatives not only uplift marginalized communities but also strengthen the social fabric by ensuring that all members of society can contribute to and benefit from economic growth. By shifting the focus from mere economic efficiency to the shared prosperity of all citizens, we pave the way for a more inclusive and just society.

Grassroots movements and community organizing play a crucial role in advancing economic justice. These efforts empower individuals to unite around common goals, fostering a sense of collective responsibility and action. By engaging in marginalized voices, these movements can effectively challenge the status quo and advocate for policies that address systemic inequities. The power of community cannot be underestimated; it is through local advocacy that we can influence broader political structures and demand change. This grassroots approach not only cultivates leadership among citizens but also builds resilient networks that can withstand the pressures of authoritarian regimes and oligarchic interests.

International organizations and coalitions are also essential in promoting economic justice on a global scale. They provide frameworks for cooperation and accountability, enabling countries to collaborate on issues such as poverty alleviation, labor rights, and environmental sustainability. By supporting international human rights standards and economic agreements that prioritize social equity, these organizations can help mitigate the adverse effects of globalization that often exacerbate inequality. Furthermore, they can hold nations accountable for their commitments to economic justice, ensuring that vulnerable populations are not left behind in the pursuit of profit.

Education is a powerful tool in the fight for economic justice. Political education and civic engagement should be integral components of our educational systems, particularly for youth. By equipping the next generation with the knowledge and skills to understand and navigate political structures, we empower them to become active participants in their democracy. This includes teaching them about the implications of oligarchy and tyranny on economic inequality and human rights. Through informed engagement, young people can challenge oppressive systems and advocate for equitable policies, creating a ripple effect that fosters a culture of justice and equality.

Finally, we must recognize the interconnectedness of economic justice and social justice. The struggle for economic equity cannot be separated from the fight for human rights, as both are essential for the thriving of a healthy society. By fostering collaboration between diverse movements—whether they focus on environmental justice, gender equality, or racial equity—we can create a more comprehensive approach to addressing systemic injustices. This holistic perspective not only strengthens our resolve but also amplifies our collective voice, ensuring that the pursuit of economic justice is at the forefront of our societal aspirations. Together, we can dismantle the structures of oppression and build a future where everyone has the opportunity to thrive.

ADVOCACY IN AUTHORITARIAN REGIMES
Challenges to Human Rights Advocacy

Challenges to human rights advocacy are multifaceted and often deeply entrenched within the political systems that govern societies. One of the most significant barriers is the existence of authoritarian regimes, where centralized power stifles dissent and limits freedoms. In these environments, advocates face the constant threat of repression, censorship, and violence. The state often deploys its resources to undermine human rights initiatives, branding them as threats to national security or social stability. This creates a climate of fear that can deter individuals from engaging in advocacy, leaving them marginalized without a voice and hindering progress toward social justice.

Moreover, economic inequality exacerbated by oligarchic structures poses another challenge to human rights advocacy. Oligarchies consolidate wealth and power among a small elite, sidelining the majority and perpetuating systemic injustices. In such settings, access to resources for advocacy efforts is severely restricted, as the wealthy elite often control the narrative and the mechanisms of change. This economic disparity creates a chasm between those who can afford to champion human rights causes and those who cannot, making it difficult for grassroots movements to gain traction. Advocates must navigate this landscape carefully, often relying on creativity and coalition-building to amplify their voices in the face of overwhelming power.

Political education and civic engagement play crucial roles in addressing these challenges. Empowering youth and communities with knowledge about their rights and the political structures that govern them can catalyze change. However, the resistance to such educational initiatives often comes from those in power, who fear an informed populace that may challenge their authority. Advocates must therefore prioritize innovative strategies to educate and mobilize individuals, fostering a culture of activism that persists even amidst adversity. The spread of technology and social media provides new platforms for advocacy, allowing for greater outreach and the potential for collective action despite oppressive conditions.

International organizations also play a pivotal role in promoting human rights, yet they face their own set of challenges. While these bodies seek to hold governments accountable, their influence can be limited by geopolitical interests and the reluctance of states to comply with international norms. Advocacy efforts often rely on the support of these organizations, but their effectiveness can vary significantly based on the political climate and the willingness of member states to engage with human rights issues. Therefore, building strong partnerships and alliances is essential to amplify the impact of advocacy on a global scale, pushing against the tide of oppression and advocating for accountability.

Ultimately, the path forward for human rights advocacy in the face of these challenges lies in resilience, solidarity, and innovation.

Advocates must remain steadfast in their commitment to justice, continually seeking new ways to confront power dynamics that threaten human rights. By fostering an inclusive movement that draws on diverse perspectives and experiences, advocates can challenge the established order and inspire a collective vision for a just society. In times of adversity, the unwavering spirit of those who fight for human rights can ignite change, proving that even the most formidable challenges can be met with hope and determination.

STRATEGIES FOR EFFECTIVE ADVOCACY

Advocacy stands as a powerful tool in the struggle for justice and equality within political systems. To wield this tool effectively, individuals must first understand the underlying structures that define their societies. Recognizing how oligarchies and tyrannies operate allows advocates to tailor their strategies to confront these systems head-on. It is essential to engage with political organizations that align with the mission of promoting human rights and social justice, as these entities are often the bedrock of meaningful change. By fostering a deep understanding of the political landscape, advocates can better navigate the complexities of their environments and amplify their voices against oppression.

One of the most effective strategies for advocacy involves building coalitions. When individuals and organizations unite under a common cause, they create a formidable force that can challenge entrenched power dynamics. Collaborating with diverse groups not only strengthens the advocacy efforts but also enriches the dialogue surrounding human rights and social justice. This coalition-building can take many forms, from grassroots movements to partnerships with international organizations. By pooling resources, knowledge, and networks, advocates can enhance their visibility and impact, making it harder for oppressive regimes to ignore their demands.

Education plays a pivotal role in effective advocacy. Political education, particularly among the youth, fosters a generation of informed citizens who are equipped to engage with their political systems. By teaching young people about their rights and responsibilities, as well as the mechanics of power, advocates can inspire a more active and engaged populace. Workshops, seminars, and community discussions can serve as platforms for disseminating knowledge about the historical context of tyranny and resistance, the impact of economic inequality, and the importance of civic engagement. An educated society is a resilient society, capable of standing firm in the face of adversity.

Harnessing the power of technology is another vital strategy for effective advocacy in contemporary society. Social media platforms and online campaigns have revolutionized the way information is disseminated and mobilized. Advocates can reach broader audiences, create awareness about human rights violations, and galvanize support for their causes. Digital tools enable real-time communication and coordination, allowing for rapid responses to emerging crises. However, this also requires a strategic approach to ensure that the messaging resonates and inspires action, particularly when addressing complex issues such as the influence of oligarchies on economic disparity or the plight of marginalized communities in authoritarian regimes.

Finally, persistence and adaptability are crucial traits for successful advocates. The landscape of political advocacy is ever-changing, influenced by shifting power dynamics, public sentiment, and global events. Advocates must remain flexible and ready to adjust their strategies as needed. This resilience, coupled with a steadfast commitment to human rights and social justice, will allow them to navigate obstacles and continue their work in promoting a healthier society. By employing these strategies, advocates can not only resist tyranny and uphold human rights but also foster an environment where democratic principles thrive and economic inequalities are addressed, ultimately contributing to a more just and equitable world.

GLOBAL SOLIDARITY AND SUPPORT

Global solidarity and support emerge as crucial pillars in the pursuit of a just and equitable world, particularly in the face of oppressive political systems. In an era where oligarchic structures often exacerbate economic inequality and authoritarian regimes stifle human rights, it becomes imperative for individuals and communities to unite across borders. This collective effort not only amplifies the voices of the marginalized but also fosters resilience against tyrannical governance. Acknowledging our shared humanity, we can draw strength from diverse experiences, creating a vibrant tapestry of solidarity that transcends geographic and cultural divides.

The call for global solidarity resonates deeply within movements advocating for human rights in authoritarian regimes. As citizens grapple with oppression, the support of the international community can serve as a formidable force against injustice. Grassroots organizations, bolstered by global networks, can mobilize resources and expertise, empowering local advocates to challenge the status quo. By shining a spotlight on human rights abuses and promoting awareness, these movements can inspire action and solidarity, demonstrating that the fight for freedom is a universal endeavor. The stories of those who have resisted tyranny remind us that courage can flourish even in the darkest times.

Political education and civic engagement are critical components of fostering global solidarity. As adults, we bear the responsibility to educate ourselves and others about the intricacies of political systems, the impact of oligarchies, and the importance of advocating for social justice. By engaging in discussions, attending workshops, and supporting educational initiatives, we can cultivate a more informed citizenry that is prepared to challenge oppressive structures. The youth, in particular, represent the future of global advocacy; thus, empowering them through education can create a ripple effect of activism that spans generations. Together, we can nurture a culture of engagement that encourages individuals to stand up for their rights and the rights of others.

International organizations play a pivotal role in promoting human rights and fostering global solidarity. Through diplomacy, advocacy, and support for local initiatives, these organizations bridge the gap between nations and create platforms for dialogue. Their influence can be instrumental in pressuring governments to uphold human rights standards and in providing assistance to those in need. By collaborating with local activists and communities, international organizations can help amplify marginalized voices, ensuring that their struggles are heard on the global stage. This partnership not only enhances the effectiveness of human rights advocacy but also reinforces the idea that we are stronger together.

In conclusion, global solidarity and support are essential in navigating the complexities of political systems and their impact on society. As we confront the challenges posed by oligarchies and authoritarian regimes, it is vital to recognize the power of collective action. By fostering a culture of understanding, advocacy, and education, we can dismantle the barriers that divide us and work towards a world where human rights are universally respected. Let us commit to standing together, not just for ourselves, but for all those who seek justice and equality, ensuring that our shared humanity triumphs over adversity.

COMPARATIVE ANALYSIS OF OLIGARCHIES AND DEMOCRACIES
Key Differences and Similarities

In the complex landscape of political systems, understanding the key differences and similarities between oligarchy and tyranny is essential for fostering a society that values human rights and social justice. Oligarchy, characterized by the concentration of power in the hands of a few, and tyranny, marked by the oppressive rule of a singular authority, both present unique challenges to democratic ideals. However, they share a common thread in their potential to undermine social equity and inhibit the collective voice of the populace. Acknowledging these dynamics empowers individuals to engage with their political environment, fostering resilience and advocacy for a just society.

One of the most striking similarities between oligarchies and tyrannies lies in their structural disregard for the democratic process. In both systems, the decision-making power is often removed from the broader citizenry, leading to a disconnect between governance and the needs of the people. This exclusion creates fertile ground for economic inequality, as policies favoring the elite are perpetuated, leaving marginalized populations vulnerable. Understanding this relationship is crucial for those advocating for human rights, as it highlights the necessity of political engagement and education in combating these disparities.

Despite their shared characteristics, oligarchies and tyrannies differ fundamentally in their methods of maintaining control. Oligarchies often operate under the guise of legitimacy, utilizing economic power and influence to shape policies while allowing for limited freedoms. In contrast, tyrannies rely on overt repression, employing fear and violence to suppress dissent. This distinction is significant for activists working within authoritarian regimes, as strategies for advocacy and resistance must be tailored to the specific nature of oppression encountered. By examining historical case studies, we can glean insights into effective approaches for challenging these systems and promoting human rights.

Moreover, the impact of international organizations in promoting human rights cannot be overstated in the context of oligarchies and tyrannies. These entities often serve as watchdogs, holding oppressive regimes accountable and supporting grassroots movements striving for change. The relationship between political systems and social justice is illuminated through the efforts of these organizations, which strive to ensure that the voices of the marginalized are heard on a global stage. Advocacy for human rights within these contexts is not only a moral imperative but a necessary component of fostering a healthy society capable of thriving despite adversity.

Ultimately, the interplay between political organizations, civic engagement, and youth education plays a pivotal role in shaping the future of our societies. By equipping the next generation with the knowledge and tools to navigate political landscapes, we can cultivate informed citizens who actively participate in democracy and challenge inequitable systems. The journey toward understanding the nuances of oligarchy and tyranny is a collective endeavor, one that requires vigilance, education, and a commitment to fostering environments where human rights are respected and upheld. As we strive for a more equitable society, recognizing these key differences and similarities will guide our efforts in promoting justice and empowering individuals to effect meaningful change.

CASE STUDIES OF SUCCESSFUL DEMOCRACIES

The study of successful democracies offers invaluable insights into the intricate tapestry of governance, showcasing how diverse political systems can foster stability, progress, and social justice. Countries such as Sweden, Canada, and New Zealand exemplify how democratic frameworks can empower citizens, promote human rights, and mitigate the risks posed by oligarchy and tyranny. These nations have not only embraced democratic principles but have also woven them into the fabric of their societies, creating environments where civic engagement and political education flourish. Such examples serve as beacons of hope, illuminating pathways toward a more equitable and just world.

In Sweden, the commitment to social welfare and equality has created a robust democracy that prioritizes the well-being of all citizens. Through progressive taxation and comprehensive social programs, the government has significantly reduced economic inequality, allowing for a more equitable distribution of resources. This model challenges the notion that economic disparity is an inevitable outcome of wealth creation, demonstrating instead that a well-structured democratic system can actively work to dismantle the foundations of oligarchy. The Swedish experience reveals that successful democracies can thrive not only on the principles of freedom and representation but also on a deep-rooted commitment to social justice.

Canada's diverse and multicultural society showcases how an inclusive democratic framework can enhance human rights advocacy, especially in the face of adversity. The nation's approach to immigration and multiculturalism has fostered a rich tapestry of voices, allowing various communities to participate actively in the political process. This inclusivity has been pivotal in addressing the needs and rights of marginalized groups, ensuring that their perspectives are not only heard but also integrated into policy-making. Canada's democratic resilience, particularly during times of crisis, underscores the importance of civic engagement and political education in nurturing a society that stands united in its commitment to human rights.

New Zealand's response to the COVID-19 pandemic serves as a powerful case study in effective governance during times of uncertainty. The government's transparent communication, swift action, and community engagement demonstrated the strength of a democratic system that prioritizes the health and safety of its citizens. By fostering trust between the government and the populace, New Zealand exemplifies how a democracy can mobilize collective action in pursuit of the common good, thereby reinforcing the vital relationship between political systems and social welfare. This approach not only mitigates the impact of crises but also strengthens the democratic fabric of society, making it more resilient against the allure of authoritarianism.

These case studies collectively illuminate the profound impact that successful democracies can have on society. By prioritizing human rights, fostering civic engagement, and promoting social justice, these nations prove that democracy is not merely a political system but a powerful tool for empowering individuals and communities. As we reflect on these examples, it becomes clear that understanding the dynamics of political systems is essential for cultivating a healthy society capable of thriving in the face of adversity. The lessons learned from these successful democracies inspire us to advocate for systems that value equality, inclusivity, and resilience, reinforcing the belief that a brighter, more just future is within our grasp.

LESSONS FROM OLIGARCHIC SYSTEMS

Understanding oligarchic systems reveals not only the intricate web of power dynamics but also the profound implications these systems have on society and individuals. Oligarchies often emerge in environments where a small group of elites consolidates power, shaping policies that benefit their interests while sidelining the majority. This concentration of power can lead to significant economic inequality, as resources and opportunities become increasingly monopolized. By analyzing these systems, we can grasp the urgent need for equitable political structures that ensure all voices are heard, advocating for a society where human rights are respected and upheld.

Oligarchic systems also serve as a stark reminder of the importance of vigilance in human rights advocacy. In many authoritarian regimes, the ruling elite often curtail freedoms and suppress dissent to maintain their grip on power. This raises a crucial challenge for civil society and international organizations: to create robust mechanisms for human rights protection. Advocacy efforts must focus on empowering marginalized groups and fostering resilience in communities facing oppression. By doing so, we not only challenge the status quo but also inspire movements that promote dignity and justice for all.

Political education and civic engagement are essential tools in countering the influence of oligarchies. When citizens are informed and engaged, they become formidable advocates for change, challenging the narratives imposed by those in power. Encouraging youth to participate in political discourse fosters a generation that values democracy and social justice, equipping them to navigate and influence the systems that govern their lives. Through education, we can cultivate critical thinkers who understand the intricacies of political organizations and their impact on policymaking, creating a more informed electorate that demands accountability from its leaders.

The interplay between political systems and social justice cannot be understated. Oligarchies often perpetuate systemic inequalities, hindering the advancement of social justice initiatives. In contrast, democratic systems, while not without flaws, offer avenues for reform and equitable representation. Comparative analyses reveal that societies thriving under democratic governance tend to prioritize inclusivity and social welfare, showcasing the transformative power of political systems that empower rather than oppress. By studying these dynamics, we can advocate for reforms that dismantle oligarchic structures and promote policies that uplift all members of society.

Finally, the role of international organizations in promoting human rights remains crucial in the face of oligarchic governance. These entities can provide support and resources to grassroots movements, amplifying the voices of those who resist tyranny. By fostering international solidarity and collaboration, we can create global networks that challenge oppressive regimes and champion human rights. The lessons drawn from oligarchic systems highlight that while the struggle for justice may be daunting, collective action, informed engagement, and unwavering commitment can pave the way for a more equitable future, inspiring hope and resilience in times of adversity.

HISTORICAL CASE STUDIES OF TYRANNY AND RESISTANCE
Lessons from History

Lessons from history reveal the intricate tapestry woven by political systems, highlighting the enduring struggle between power and justice. The rise and fall of various regimes illuminate the consequences of unchecked authority, as seen in the tyrannies that have marked human civilization. These lessons remind us of the critical need for vigilance and engagement in our political landscapes. By examining past events, we glean insights into how societies can thrive or falter based on the structures governing them, urging us to remain committed to building equitable systems that uphold human dignity and rights.

Oligarchies have historically exacerbated economic inequality, concentrating wealth and power in the hands of a few while leaving the majority marginalized. The case of ancient Rome serves as a stark example; as power became centralized among elite families, the gap between the affluent and the poor widened, leading to social unrest and eventual collapse. This historical perspective underscores the importance of advocating for systems that promote economic justice and equitable distribution of resources. By learning from these disparities, we can devise strategies to challenge oligarchic tendencies in contemporary societies, fostering a climate where opportunity is accessible to all.

Human rights advocacy in authoritarian regimes often emerges from the ashes of resistance. The narratives of activists who bravely confronted oppressive governments remind us that the fight for dignity and freedom is timeless. Historical figures such as Nelson Mandela and Aung San Suu Kyi exemplify the power of resilience against tyranny, illustrating the profound impact individuals can have when they stand for justice. Their stories inspire current and future generations to engage in human rights advocacy, emphasizing that even in the darkest times, hope and courage can pave the way for transformative change.

Political education and civic engagement are essential for young people to navigate the complexities of modern governance. Historical movements reveal that informed citizens are the backbone of thriving democracies. The civil rights movement in the United States serves as a powerful testament to the impact of collective action driven by an informed populace. By investing in the political education of youth, we empower them to challenge systemic injustices and advocate for social change. This foundation of knowledge fosters a new generation of leaders who will champion human rights and ensure that the lessons of history are not forgotten.

The role of international organizations in promoting human rights cannot be overstated. Historical examples, such as the establishment of the United Nations after World War II, illustrate the global commitment to uphold human dignity. These organizations serve as platforms for collaboration and advocacy, providing support to those fighting against oppression. As we reflect on their influence, we must recognize the importance of solidarity across borders, uniting to promote social justice and human rights worldwide. By learning from the past and actively participating in these global efforts, we can foster a healthier society that thrives even in times of adversity.

NOTABLE RESISTANCE MOVEMENTS

Notable resistance movements throughout history have served as pivotal examples of the struggle against oppressive political systems. These movements, often born from the ashes of tyranny and oligarchy, highlight the resilience of the human spirit and the unyielding quest for justice and equality. From the civil rights movement in the United States to the anti-apartheid struggle in South Africa, these efforts not only sought to dismantle oppressive regimes but also aimed to reshape societal norms and values, proving that collective action can indeed alter the course of history.

The civil rights movement of the 1960s stands as a beacon of hope and courage in the face of systemic racism and discrimination. Led by figures such as Martin Luther King Jr., this movement galvanized individuals from diverse backgrounds to stand united against injustice. Through peaceful protests, sit-ins, and powerful speeches, activists challenged the status quo and demanded equal rights for African Americans. The passage of landmark legislation, such as the Civil Rights Act of 1964, was not merely a political victory but a testament to the power of organized resistance and civic engagement. This movement underscores the importance of political education and the role of grassroots organizations in advocating for human rights.

In South Africa, the anti-apartheid movement exemplified the struggle against a deeply entrenched system of racial segregation and oppression. Led by figures like Nelson Mandela, this movement harnessed the power of both peaceful protest and armed resistance to challenge the apartheid regime. The international community's support, including economic sanctions and advocacy from various organizations, played a crucial role in amplifying the voices of the oppressed. The eventual dismantling of apartheid in the early 1990s not only marked a significant victory for human rights but also served as a reminder of the global interconnectedness of resistance movements. It highlighted the importance of solidarity and international cooperation in the fight against injustice.

The Arab Spring serves as a contemporary example of resistance against authoritarian regimes across the Middle East and North Africa. Sparked by widespread discontent with corruption, economic inequality, and lack of political freedom, citizens took to the streets demanding change. Social media played a critical role in organizing protests and disseminating information, empowering ordinary people to challenge long-standing power structures. While the outcomes of these uprisings varied, they undeniably altered the political landscape and inspired future generations to engage in civic activism. The Arab Spring illustrates the potential for grassroots movements to foster dialogue around social justice and human rights, even in the face of formidable opposition.

In examining these notable resistance movements, it becomes evident that the struggle for justice is often interwoven with the fight against economic inequality and the advocacy for human rights. Each movement, while unique in its context and methods, shares common threads of resilience, solidarity, and an unwavering belief in the possibility of change. Such movements remind us that when individuals unite against oppressive systems, they can challenge and transform the very foundations of society. By studying these historical cases, we not only honor those who fought for justice but also equip ourselves to support contemporary efforts aimed at fostering a healthy and equitable society.

THE INNER DESIRE FOR FULFILLMENT
Understanding Our Natural Human Structure

Understanding our natural human structure is fundamental to reimagining democracy and embracing the potential for social change. At the core of our being lies a complex interplay of emotions, desires, and aspirations that shape our interactions with one another and the systems we inhabit. This intrinsic design compels us toward connection, compassion, and collaboration. However, the societal structures that often govern our lives can stifle these natural inclinations, leading to discontent and a sense of disconnection. By recognizing and understanding our inherent human nature, we can begin to envision a democracy that aligns with our deepest values and promotes genuine fulfillment.

The philosophy of politics and social change must engage with the essence of individual agency. Each person possesses a unique voice and perspective, contributing to the broader narrative of society. When individuals harness their agency, they unleash a powerful force capable of challenging the status quo. The role of non-conformity becomes crucial, as it acts as a catalyst for transformation. Those who dare to question prevailing norms often inspire others to do the same, creating a ripple effect that can reshape political landscapes. Embracing this non-conformity is not merely an act of rebellion; it is an affirmation of our shared humanity and a step toward a more inclusive and equitable society.

Existentialism intersects profoundly with political activism, urging us to confront the realities of existence and our responsibilities within the communal framework. The acknowledgment of our freedom and the weight of our choices can lead to greater empathy and a commitment to social justice. This philosophical approach encourages individuals to engage in meaningful actions that reflect their values, bridging the gap between personal fulfillment and the collective good. As we navigate the complexities of our lives, the call to action becomes not just a political imperative but a moral one, reinforcing the idea that our struggles for freedom and justice are intertwined.

Alternative lifestyles present a compelling response to the constraints of mainstream society. By choosing paths that honor our authentic selves, we challenge the dominant narratives that dictate how we should live, work, and engage with one another. These alternatives often embody principles of sustainability, community, and mindfulness, fostering environments where personal fulfillment can flourish alongside social responsibility. As we explore these unconventional ways of living, we can cultivate a deeper understanding of happiness that transcends material success, emphasizing instead the richness of shared experiences and collective well-being.

In this landscape of reimagined democracy, the ethics of dissent and civil disobedience emerge as vital components of social change. When individuals stand up against injustice, they not only assert their rights but also awaken the collective conscience of society. Mindfulness practices can enhance this engagement, fostering awareness of the interconnectedness of our lives and the impact of our actions. Ultimately, by understanding our natural human structure and embracing our capacity for agency, we can cultivate a transformative movement that honors both personal and community aspirations, paving the way for a more equitable and fulfilling future for all.

SOCIETAL OPPOSITION TO INDIVIDUAL NEEDS

In contemporary society, the tension between individual needs and societal expectations often manifests as a profound conflict, one that challenges the very foundations of democracy. Individuals frequently find themselves at odds with the prevailing norms and structures that govern collective life. This opposition can stifle personal growth and fulfillment, leading people to question their place within a system that appears to prioritize conformity over authenticity. Yet, the path to a more meaningful existence lies in recognizing and confronting these societal constraints, urging us to embrace our unique identities and aspirations.

The philosophy of politics and social change invites us to explore the intricate relationship between individual agency and collective action. Each person's voice carries the potential to resonate within the greater social fabric, fostering movements that advocate for justice and equity. When individuals assert their needs and desires, they not only reclaim their agency but also inspire others to do the same. This shared journey toward self-actualization can ignite transformative social movements, proving that dissent is not merely a reaction to oppression but a vital expression of humanity's collective aspiration for a better world.

Non-conformity emerges as a powerful catalyst for political systems that often resist change. Those who dare to challenge the status quo embody the spirit of existentialism, driving forward the belief that authenticity is paramount. They remind us that each act of rebellion—

be it through art, activism, or lifestyle choices—serves as a poignant critique of societal norms. By stepping outside the confines of conventional behavior, these individuals illuminate alternative pathways to fulfillment, encouraging others to question the very principles that govern their lives.

As we navigate the complexities of modern existence, alternative lifestyles become essential responses to mainstream societal pressures. These choices, often viewed as radical, reflect a deeper yearning for connection, purpose, and joy. In embracing unconventional living, individuals not only carve out spaces for their own happiness but also challenge the broader community to reconsider its values. This process of reimagining happiness through the lens of social justice emphasizes that true contentment arises not just from personal achievements but from the well-being of the collective.

Ultimately, the interplay between personal fulfillment and community well-being is a dynamic that defines our shared humanity. As mindfulness practices gain traction in political engagement, individuals learn to cultivate awareness of their own needs while remaining attuned to the struggles of others. This synthesis of self-care and social responsibility fosters a culture of empathy and support, enabling us to reimagine democracy as a living, breathing entity. By embracing unconventional philosophies and championing the individual within the collective, we can pave the way for a society that honors both the inner desires of its members and the greater good.

INDIVIDUAL AGENCY IN SOCIAL MOVEMENTS
The Role of the Individual in Collective Action

STORIES OF EMPOWERMENT AND CHANGE

In the quest for social change, stories of empowerment resonate with the heartbeat of humanity, illuminating the transformative power of individual agency. Consider the tale of a small community that faced systemic injustice. With a handful of determined individuals, the seeds of dissent were planted. They gathered not only to voice their grievances but to share their visions of a life rooted in fulfillment and harmony. This grassroots movement, fueled by a collective yearning for a better society, blossomed into a vibrant tapestry of voices that challenged the status quo. Each participant brought their unique perspective, embodying the essence of non-conformity and proving that even the smallest actions can ripple through the fabric of society, sparking profound change.

Empowerment often arises from the intersection of personal struggle and collective action. Take, for instance, the story of a single mother who, after facing discrimination in the workplace, decided to challenge the existing norms. Rather than retreating into despair, she rallied others who shared her plight, creating a network that advocated for fair labor practices. Through her journey, she discovered that her individual experience was part of a larger narrative—one that questioned the ethical foundations of her community. By embracing her voice, she not only uplifted herself but also ignited a movement that encouraged countless others to confront their own challenges. This intertwining of personal fulfillment and community well-being reveals how individual agency can catalyze systemic change.

Existentialism teaches us that our existence is defined by our actions and choices. This philosophy becomes profoundly relevant when examining social movements. Activists who embrace existential principles often navigate the complexities of their own desires while challenging societal norms. One compelling example is the rise of alternative lifestyles as a form of political engagement. Individuals living authentically, whether through sustainable farming, communal living, or artistic expression, embody a rejection of mainstream values that prioritize consumption over connection. Their commitment to living in alignment with their beliefs not only fulfills their inner desires but also serves as a powerful critique of the prevailing political systems, inspiring others to reevaluate their own paths.

The ethics of dissent and civil disobedience play a crucial role in stories of empowerment. History is replete with individuals who choose to stand against injustice, often at great personal risk. Their acts of bravery remind us that dissent is not merely an act of rebellion; it is a profound expression of hope. From peaceful protests to powerful speeches, these moments of courage galvanize communities and awaken a collective consciousness. The influence of mindfulness in these actions cannot be understated; when individuals engage thoughtfully and intentionally with their dissent, they cultivate a deeper understanding of their impact, transforming frustration into purposeful action. This mindful approach fosters resilience and commitment, essential ingredients for any movement seeking to reimagine democracy.

Ultimately, the stories of empowerment and change reflect an unwavering belief in the possibility of a better world. They reveal that the pursuit of happiness is intricately linked to social justice, challenging us to redefine our understanding of fulfillment. By embracing unconventional philosophies and acknowledging the interconnectedness of our lives, we can cultivate a society that honors both individual aspirations and collective well-being. These narratives inspire us to envision a future where every voice matters, urging us to engage in the ongoing dialogue of democracy reimagined. Through empowerment, we find not only the strength to effect change but also the courage to live authentically in a world that often resists our true nature.

NON-CONFORMITY AND POLITICAL SYSTEMS
The Impact of Divergence on Governance

Divergence, as a concept, embodies the essence of individuality and the myriad expressions of human experience. In the realm of governance, this divergence manifests in the varied ideologies, practices, and policies that emerge when diverse voices are acknowledged and celebrated. When the structures of power are receptive to the unique perspectives of their constituents, they cultivate an environment where creativity flourishes, leading to innovative solutions that address the complexities of contemporary society. This impact of divergence on governance is not merely a theoretical construct; it is a transformative force that empowers individuals to reclaim their agency and reshape the systems that govern their lives.

The recognition of divergent viewpoints can catalyze profound social change. When traditional governance models rigidly adhere to conformity, they stifle the potential for progress and entrench inequalities. Conversely, embracing non-conformity encourages a dynamic political landscape where marginalized voices rise and contribute to a richer discourse. This shift not only revitalizes the political arena but also fosters a culture of inclusivity, where individuals feel a sense of belonging and responsibility towards each other. Such an environment nurtures collective action, encouraging citizens to engage in social movements that reflect their values and aspirations, ultimately leading to a more equitable society.

Existentialism plays a pivotal role in this exploration of divergence within governance. By emphasizing individual choice and the search for meaning, existentialist philosophy invites us to question established norms and the status quo. In the context of political activism, this philosophical framework empowers individuals to assert their beliefs and challenge oppressive systems. The act of dissent becomes a manifestation of personal authenticity and a commitment to societal betterment. As people align their inner desires with collective goals, they create a powerful synergy that can disrupt entrenched power dynamics and pave the way for transformative change.

Moreover, alternative lifestyles serve as a tangible response to the failings of mainstream society. By choosing paths that diverge from conventional expectations, individuals not only enhance their personal fulfillment but also model new ways of living that prioritize community well-being. These lifestyles challenge the dominant narratives of success and happiness, revealing that true fulfillment often lies in connection, creativity, and compassion. As more individuals embrace these alternative ways of living, they collectively contribute to a broader reimagining of governance that values emotional and social intelligence alongside economic metrics.

Ultimately, the impact of divergence on governance is intricately tied to the philosophy of happiness within the context of social justice. A society that prioritizes the well-being of its citizens must foster an environment where diverse perspectives are not only heard but celebrated. The ethics of dissent and civil disobedience become essential tools for those striving for a more just world. By cultivating mindfulness and a sense of community, individuals can engage more meaningfully in political processes, ensuring that governance reflects the rich tapestry of human experience. In this reimagined democracy, the embrace of divergence transforms not just the structures of power, but the very fabric of society itself, leading us toward a brighter, more inclusive future.

CASE STUDIES OF NON-CONFORMIST MOVEMENTS

The exploration of non-conformist movements reveals a rich tapestry woven from threads of individual agency, existential thought, and a fervent desire for social change. These movements often arise from a deep-seated recognition that existing political systems may not adequately reflect the inner truths of humanity. Take, for instance, the Beat Generation of the 1950s. This group of writers and artists rejected mainstream values, advocating for personal liberation through creative expression, spirituality, and an embrace of alternative lifestyles. Their willingness to challenge societal norms sparked a cultural revolution that influenced countless individuals to reconsider their own paths, encouraging a profound shift in the collective consciousness towards authenticity and connection.

Another powerful example is the Civil Rights Movement, which epitomized the intersection of individual agency and collective action. Figures like Martin Luther King Jr. and Rosa Parks exemplified how personal conviction can ignite widespread social change. By engaging in acts of civil disobedience, they challenged an oppressive system, demonstrating that non-conformity could serve as a catalyst for justice. Their legacy teaches us that dissent is not only a right but a moral responsibility, reminding us that the struggle for equality and dignity is woven into the very fabric of democratic ideals. This movement underscores the importance of understanding one's own agency in the face of systemic obstacles and emphasizes the potential for individual actions to resonate on a larger scale.

The rise of environmental activism in recent decades showcases how non-conformity can reshape political discourse. Groups like Extinction Rebellion and the youth-led Fridays for Future movement challenge the status quo by advocating for sustainability and climate justice. Their approach often incorporates existential themes, urging society to confront the fundamental questions of existence and our responsibilities to future generations. These activists embody the idea that living in alignment with one's values can inspire others to join the fight against environmental degradation, illustrating that personal fulfillment and community well-being are deeply entwined. By embracing alternative lifestyles and advocating for systemic change, they provide a blueprint for those seeking a more harmonious relationship with the planet.

In the realm of mindfulness and political engagement, movements such as the Mindfulness Revolution have emerged as a response to societal discontent. By promoting practices that foster awareness and compassion, these initiatives encourage individuals to reflect on their roles within the larger social landscape. The intersection of mindfulness and activism underscores the importance of inner peace as a foundation for meaningful social change. Individuals who cultivate a mindful approach are more likely to engage thoughtfully with the complexities of political systems, fostering a sense of agency that can lead to transformative action. This synergy between personal growth and collective responsibility holds the potential to reimagine democracy in ways that honor both individual desires and community needs.

Ultimately, the case studies of non-conformist movements illuminate the profound impact of alternative philosophies on the progression of society. They invite us to envision a democracy that is not only responsive to the voices of the marginalized but also nurturing of the individual spirit. In a world that often feels at odds with our inner nature, these movements remind us of the power of dissent and the importance of living authentically. As we reflect on these examples, we are inspired to embrace our own non-conformist tendencies, recognizing that the journey towards a more just and fulfilling society begins with each of us daring to envision a different future.

EXISTENTIALISM AND POLITICAL ACTIVISM
The Intersection of Meaning and Action

At the heart of social change lies a profound relationship between meaning and action, where the ideals we hold shape the pursuits we undertake. In a world often dictated by routine and conformity, individuals are called to find personal significance in their actions, fostering a sense of purpose that transcends the superficial norms imposed by society. This intersection invites us to explore how deeply held beliefs can catalyze transformative movements, as individuals become not merely passive observers but active creators of their realities. By embracing this philosophy, we tap into the essence of democracy itself, encouraging a vibrant tapestry of voices to emerge from the shadows of indifference.

Understanding the power of individual agency is crucial in this exploration. Each person's choices, influenced by their unique understanding of meaning, contribute to a collective narrative that can challenge oppressive systems. When individuals recognize their capacity to effect change, they become empowered to act against injustices, motivated by their personal experiences and convictions. This realization ignites a spark of non-conformity that can disrupt the status quo, fostering a culture where dissent is not only accepted but celebrated. As we navigate the complexities of political landscapes, it is this very agency that forms the backbone of social movements, driving them forward with passion and resilience.

Existentialism, with its emphasis on authenticity and individual freedom, provides a rich philosophical backdrop for political activism. It teaches us that our existence precedes our essence; thus, the choices we make are imbued with meaning that can resonate beyond our immediate surroundings. Activists who embody this philosophy understand that their struggles are not isolated but rather part of a larger human experience, echoing the desires and aspirations of countless others. This perspective transforms activism from mere action into a profound expression of humanity's quest for meaning, inviting others to join in a shared pursuit of justice and fulfillment.

Alternative lifestyles often emerge as powerful responses to mainstream societal norms, offering individuals a way to align their lives with their values. These unconventional paths challenge the prevailing narratives of success and happiness, proposing that true fulfillment comes from authentic engagement with the world. By choosing to live differently, individuals demonstrate that societal change begins with personal transformation. This alignment of values and actions creates ripples of influence, inspiring communities to rethink their priorities and embrace a more holistic understanding of well-being that prioritizes collective happiness over individual gain.

In this intricate dance between meaning and action, mindfulness plays a pivotal role in shaping our political engagement. By cultivating awareness of our thoughts and intentions, we can better navigate the complexities of dissent and civil disobedience, ensuring our actions are rooted in ethical considerations. This conscious approach to activism not only enhances our understanding of our impact but also strengthens our commitment to the ideals we champion. As we reimagine democracy through these unconventional lenses, we discover the profound interconnectedness of personal fulfillment and

community well-being, creating a more just and vibrant society that honors the diverse tapestry of human experience.

EXISTENTIAL PHILOSOPHERS AND THEIR INFLUENCE

Existential philosophers have long grappled with the profound complexities of human existence, and their insights hold a transformative potential for contemporary democracy. Thinkers such as Jean-Paul Sartre, Simone de Beauvoir, and Albert Camus emphasized the importance of individual agency, arguing that each person has the power—and the responsibility—to shape their own destiny. In a world often characterized by conformity and societal pressures, these philosophers remind us that embracing our freedom can lead to more authentic lives. This existential awareness sparks a desire for social change, urging individuals to recognize their role in shaping a more just society.

The influence of existential thought on political activism is undeniable. Sartre's notion that "existence precedes essence" empowers individuals to reject predetermined identities and societal roles. This rejection fosters a spirit of non-conformity, which can disrupt oppressive political systems. When individuals assert their agency and challenge the status quo, they inspire collective movements that seek to redefine justice and equality. The existentialist emphasis on personal responsibility becomes a catalyst for social change, encouraging individuals to act in alignment with their values and to advocate for a society that reflects their vision of fulfillment and happiness.

Simone de Beauvoir's exploration of freedom and ethics provides a compelling framework for understanding the relationship between personal fulfillment and community well-being. Her assertion that "one is not born, but rather becomes a woman" highlights the fluidity of identity and the importance of social structures in shaping our experiences. By recognizing the interconnectedness of individual and collective identities, we can cultivate alternative lifestyles that challenge mainstream norms. These lifestyles not only serve as personal expressions of authenticity but also as radical acts of resistance against a society that often stifles true human potential.

Civil disobedience, as articulated by existentialists, emerges as a powerful ethical stance against injustice. Figures like Camus championed the idea of the absurd, which compels individuals to confront the meaninglessness of life and, in doing so, find the courage to resist oppressive systems. This philosophy encourages citizens to engage in acts of dissent that align with their moral convictions. The ethics of dissent becomes a pathway for individuals to assert their beliefs, fostering a culture of mindfulness in political engagement. Such mindfulness not only enhances personal fulfillment but also strengthens the fabric of community well-being by promoting active participation and solidarity.

Ultimately, the intersection of existentialism and democracy invites us to reimagine our political landscape through unconventional perspectives. By embracing existential thought, we can cultivate a deeper understanding of happiness in the context of social justice. This journey involves recognizing the inherent value of individual agency while simultaneously acknowledging our shared responsibility to foster a more equitable society. As we embody the principles of existentialism, we empower ourselves and others to engage with life meaningfully, transforming our communities and our world in the quest for a more fulfilling existence.

ALTERNATIVE LIFESTYLES AS RESISTANCE
Exploring Counter-Cultural Movements

Counter-cultural movements have long served as catalysts for profound change, challenging the status quo and urging society to reexamine its values and practices. These movements often emerge in response to perceived injustices, drawing individuals who feel alienated by mainstream ideologies. By embracing alternative lifestyles and philosophies, participants in these movements create a space where individual agency flourishes, fostering an environment ripe for social transformation. This exploration of counter-culture reveals how the quest for personal fulfillment intertwines with broader societal aspirations, ultimately reshaping our understanding of democracy.

At the heart of counter-cultural movements lies the desire for authenticity and connection. Individuals often find themselves at odds with societal norms that prioritize conformity over individuality. By rejecting these constraints, they assert their right to exist outside conventional frameworks. This rebellion not only empowers personal freedom but also inspires collective action, demonstrating the profound impact of non-conformity on political systems. When individuals band together to express their dissent, they challenge the dominant narratives that dictate the terms of engagement in a democratic society.

The intersection of existentialism and political activism illuminates the philosophical underpinnings of counter-cultural movements. Existentialist thought emphasizes the importance of personal choice and responsibility, encouraging individuals to seek meaning in their lives despite societal pressures. This philosophy resonates deeply within counter-culture, as activists embrace the idea that their actions can lead to significant social change. By confronting existential dilemmas head-on, they cultivate a sense of agency that propels them toward activism, transforming personal struggles into a collective push for justice and equity.

Alternative lifestyles often emerge as a direct response to the discontent with mainstream society. These lifestyles are not merely escapist retreats; they represent intentional choices aimed at fostering community, sustainability, and social justice. From communal living arrangements to eco-conscious practices, such alternatives challenge the dominant consumerist culture and advocate for a more harmonious existence with nature. This shift towards mindful living reflects a growing recognition of the interconnectedness of personal fulfillment and community well-being, suggesting that true happiness is rooted in our relationships with others and the world around us.

As we reflect on the ethics of dissent and civil disobedience, we recognize the vital role these actions play in shaping a more equitable society. Mindfulness, too, has emerged as a powerful tool for political engagement, allowing individuals to align their inner values with their outer actions. By cultivating awareness and compassion, activists can navigate the complexities of dissent with integrity and purpose. Ultimately, exploring counter-cultural movements invites us to reimagine democracy through unconventional perspectives, drawing from ancient philosophies that have long advocated for justice and human dignity. Through this lens, we can embrace a future where individual agency and collective aspiration coalesce, forging a path toward a more fulfilling existence for all.

THE INFLUENCE OF INTENTIONAL COMMUNITIES

The influence of intentional communities resonates deeply within the fabric of social change, offering a powerful counter-narrative to the mainstream societal structures that often stifle individual expression and fulfillment. These communities, formed around shared values and a common purpose, provide a living testament to the potential of collective action grounded in intentionality. By embracing alternative lifestyles and non-conformity, individuals find refuge and empowerment, cultivating environments where personal agency can flourish alongside communal well-being. In this light, intentional communities serve as incubators for innovative ideas and practices that challenge conventional political systems, advocating for a democracy that is participatory and inclusive.

As individuals engage in these communities, they often discover an enhanced sense of agency that transcends the limitations imposed by traditional societal roles. This realization fosters a profound connection between personal fulfillment and collective action, where the pursuit of happiness becomes intertwined with the well-being of the community. The shared experiences and mutual support found in these settings encourage members to explore their existential concerns within a framework of collaboration and solidarity. The impact of this interconnectedness is transformative, igniting a passion for activism that is both deeply personal and profoundly political.

Intentional communities not only provide a space for individual growth but also challenge the very foundations of societal norms. By existing outside the mainstream, they demonstrate that alternative lifestyles can yield innovative solutions to pressing social issues. These communities often embody principles of sustainability, equity, and justice, which resonate with the ethical imperatives of dissent and civil disobedience. Through their practices, members illustrate that the act of living differently is a form of protest against systems that perpetuate inequality and alienation, thereby reimagining the possibilities of democracy as a living practice rather than a static ideal.

The philosophy of happiness, particularly in the context of social justice, finds fertile ground within intentional communities. Members often engage in mindful practices that not only enhance personal well-being but also cultivate a culture of care and responsibility toward one another. This mindfulness creates a space where political engagement becomes a natural extension of personal fulfillment, reinforcing the idea that true democracy is rooted in the health of its communities. By prioritizing relationships and collective well-being, these communities challenge the pervasive notion that individual success must come at the expense of others.

Ultimately, the influence of intentional communities extends far beyond their immediate members, offering a blueprint for reimagining democracy itself. Through their commitment to alternative philosophies and practices, they inspire a wider movement toward social change that values diversity, inclusivity, and empathy. In a world often marked by division and disillusionment, these communities shine as beacons of hope, illuminating the path toward a more equitable and fulfilling existence. By embracing the lessons of intentional living, we can collectively forge a society that honors our shared humanity, fostering a democracy that is vibrant, resilient, and truly reflective of the diverse voices that comprise it.

THE PHILOSOPHY OF HAPPINESS AND SOCIAL JUSTICE

Redefining Happiness in a Social Context

Happiness, often perceived as a personal pursuit, takes on a different hue when placed within a social context. In a world increasingly defined by its complexities and challenges, redefining happiness means recognizing it as a collective experience intertwined with the fabric of society. This shift urges us to look beyond the individualistic lens that has long dominated our understanding of fulfillment. Instead, we must explore how our happiness is deeply connected to the wellbeing of others, suggesting that the true essence of joy lies in our shared experiences and mutual support. By embracing this interconnectedness, we can foster a more compassionate society that values collective flourishing.

The philosophy of happiness in the context of social justice serves as a vital framework for understanding this connection. Happiness cannot exist in a vacuum, especially when systemic inequalities persist. When individuals experience oppression or disenfranchisement, their capacity for happiness diminishes, not just for themselves but for the community at large. Therefore, seeking justice and advocating for equitable systems is not merely a political act; it is a moral imperative that enhances our collective happiness. In this sense, our pursuit of personal fulfillment must align with the broader goal of creating a society that nurtures the potential of all its members, allowing happiness to blossom in a more inclusive environment.

Moreover, the role of individual agency in social movements cannot be overstated. Each person possesses the power to influence change and contribute to a collective vision of happiness. This empowerment is crucial, as it encourages individuals to step outside the confines of conformity and engage actively in the political landscape. Non-conformity, often viewed with skepticism, can actually serve as a catalyst for revolutionary ideas and practices that challenge the status quo. By embracing our unique perspectives and experiences, we enrich the dialogue on happiness, highlighting diverse pathways to fulfillment that resonate across different communities.

The intersection of existentialism and political activism further emphasizes the importance of redefining happiness. At its core, existentialism challenges us to find meaning in our choices and actions. When we engage in political activism, we confront the absurdities of life and assert our existence through purposeful action. This engagement not only enriches our personal lives but also contributes to a broader narrative of social change. As we fight for justice, we cultivate a sense of belonging and purpose that transcends individual concerns, ultimately reinforcing the idea that happiness is most profound when shared with others in the pursuit of a common cause.

In this landscape of redefined happiness, alternative lifestyles emerge as powerful responses to mainstream societal norms. These lifestyles challenge the conventional definitions of success and fulfillment, advocating for a more authentic existence rooted in community, mindfulness, and ethical living. By prioritizing relationships over materialism, we nurture a culture that values connection and empathy, essential ingredients for a happy society. As we reimagine democracy through unconventional perspectives, we pave the way for a future where happiness is not just an individual pursuit but a collective journey toward a more just and fulfilling world for all.

THE PURSUIT OF JUSTICE AS A PATH TO FULFILLMENT

The pursuit of justice is not merely a political endeavor; it is a deeply personal journey that intertwines with our quest for fulfillment. In a world often marked by inequality and oppression, the call to seek justice resonates with the very core of our humanity. This inner drive compels us to engage with societal issues, not just as citizens but as individuals seeking a more meaningful existence. By aligning our personal values with the collective struggles for justice, we discover a profound sense of purpose. Each act of advocacy, however small, serves as a step towards not only transforming society but also enriching our own inner lives.

Engaging in the pursuit of justice fosters a sense of agency that is essential for individual growth. In this act of standing up against injustice, we reclaim our power and affirm our capacity to effect change. This empowerment is transformative; it allows us to transcend feelings of helplessness that often accompany societal challenges. When individuals take a stand—whether through protest, advocacy, or community organizing—they not only contribute to a larger movement but also nurture their own self-worth and identity. This interplay between personal agency and collective action illustrates how the fight for justice can lead to unparalleled personal fulfillment.

Non-conformity emerges as a powerful catalyst for both social change and personal liberation. By challenging conventional norms and expectations, individuals embrace their uniqueness and contribute to a richer tapestry of activism. This divergence from the status quo invites a deeper exploration of values and beliefs, encouraging individuals to forge paths that resonate with their true selves. As we step away from the pressures of conformity, we not only advocate for justice but also inspire others to embark on their journeys of self-discovery. In this way, the pursuit of justice becomes a collective narrative of resilience and authenticity, where the act of dissent is celebrated as a vital expression of the human spirit.

Existentialism provides a fertile ground for understanding the relationship between personal fulfillment and social activism. It reminds us that our existence precedes essence, allowing us the freedom to define our purpose. Engaging with social justice issues can be seen as a conscious choice to live authentically, making decisions that reflect our values and beliefs. This existential commitment to justice fosters a sense of belonging and connection to something greater than oneself. When individuals embrace their roles as agents of change, they not only pursue justice for others but also carve out a meaningful existence that aligns with their deepest convictions.

Ultimately, the pursuit of justice is a journey toward a more fulfilling life that transcends personal aspirations and nurtures communal well-being. As we engage with social movements, we cultivate relationships that enrich our lives and foster a sense of belonging. This interconnectedness reinforces the idea that individual happiness is intricately linked to the health of our communities. In reimagining democracy through unconventional philosophies, we recognize that the path to fulfillment is paved with acts of courage, compassion, and commitment to justice. By embracing this journey, we not only advocate for change but also awaken the profound potential within ourselves and the world around us.

ETHICS OF DISSENT AND CIVIL DISOBEDIENCE

Philosophical Foundations of Dissent

Dissent has always been a fundamental aspect of political and social evolution, rooted deeply in the philosophical traditions that seek to understand the nature of human existence and societal structures. At its core, dissent challenges the status quo, compelling individuals to question the accepted narratives that define their lives. This act of defiance can emerge from a profound realization that societal norms often conflict with the intrinsic values of humanity, such as freedom, justice, and equality. Philosophers throughout history, from Socrates to Rousseau, have illuminated the necessity of dissent as a catalyst for personal and collective growth, urging individuals to embrace their inner voices in the pursuit of a more fulfilling existence.

Existentialism, as a philosophical movement, underscores the significance of individual agency in the quest for authenticity. Thinkers like Sartre and Camus posited that individuals must confront the absurdity of life and take responsibility for crafting their own meanings. This perspective resonates deeply within social movements that advocate for change, as it encourages individuals to transcend societal expectations and assert their unique identities. Dissent, in this context, becomes a powerful expression of personal autonomy, allowing people to reclaim their narratives and inspire others to do the same. By embracing existentialist thought, activists can nurture a sense of purpose that propels them toward social justice, fostering an environment where dissent is not merely tolerated but celebrated.

The intersection of non-conformity and political systems reveals the transformative potential of dissent. Non-conformists challenge the rigidity of established power structures, exposing inherent injustices and inequalities. History offers numerous examples where the refusal to conform has led to significant societal shifts, from the civil rights movement to contemporary climate activism. These movements illustrate how dissent can galvanize communities, drawing together individuals united by a shared vision of a better world. The act of standing apart from the crowd not only empowers dissenters but also inspires others to critically examine their beliefs and engage in collective action, thereby reshaping the political landscape.

Moreover, the philosophy of happiness plays an essential role in understanding the ethics of dissent. Happiness, often viewed as a personal pursuit, is intricately linked to social justice and community well-being. Engaging in acts of dissent can foster a deeper sense of fulfillment, as individuals align their actions with their values and contribute to the greater good. This alignment brings about a profound realization that true happiness is not found in conformity or complacency, but in actively participating in the shaping of a just society. As individuals advocate for change, they not only seek to improve their circumstances but also work toward the collective happiness of their communities, illustrating the ethical dimension of dissent.

Ultimately, reimagining democracy through unconventional philosophies invites a holistic approach to political engagement. Mindfulness, for instance, can enhance one's awareness of the socio-political landscape, fostering a deeper understanding of the complexities of dissent. By cultivating a mindful practice, individuals can engage more thoughtfully in political discourse, ensuring their dissent is rooted in compassion and empathy. This mindful engagement encourages a redefinition of democracy, one that values diverse perspectives and nurtures the human spirit. As we embrace the philosophical foundations of dissent, we embark on a transformative journey that not only challenges societal norms but also allows us to realize our fullest potential as agents of change.

HISTORICAL EXAMPLES OF ETHICAL RESISTANCE

Throughout history, individuals and collectives have demonstrated remarkable ethical resistance against oppressive systems, embodying the essence of courage and conviction. These historical examples serve not only as a testament to the power of individual agency but also illuminate the profound impact of non-conformity in shaping political landscapes. From the abolitionists who fought against slavery in the United States to the suffragists advocating for women's rights, these movements remind us that the desire for a more just society is deeply rooted in our humanity. In these narratives, we find inspiration and a call to embrace our own capacity for dissent as a means of fostering social change.

One of the most compelling instances of ethical resistance can be traced back to Mahatma Gandhi's philosophy of nonviolent protest. His commitment to civil disobedience and satyagraha not only challenged British colonial rule in India but also inspired global movements for civil rights and freedom. Gandhi's approach exemplified the intersection of existentialism and political activism, as he emphasized the importance of personal integrity and moral conviction in the face of systemic injustice. His life serves as a reminder that ethical resistance is not merely a political act but a profound expression of one's inner values and the pursuit of a more fulfilling existence aligned with the principles of justice and equality.

Similarly, the civil rights movement in the United States showcased the powerful role of individual agency in dismantling segregation and discrimination. Figures like Martin Luther King Jr. and Rosa Parks emerged as beacons of hope, employing strategies of nonviolent resistance and civil disobedience to challenge deeply entrenched societal norms. Their actions not only transformed the political landscape but also ignited a collective consciousness that emphasized the interconnectedness of personal fulfillment and community well-being. The movement illustrated that ethical resistance is a communal endeavor, where individual acts of courage resonate and inspire collective action toward a more equitable society.

In more recent history, the LGBTQ+ rights movement exemplifies the impact of non-conformity on political systems. Activists like Marsha P. Johnson and Harvey Milk dared to defy societal expectations and advocate for love and acceptance in the face of widespread discrimination. Their struggles not only advanced legal rights but also fostered a cultural shift that embraced diversity and challenged conventional norms. This movement underscores the notion that alternative lifestyles can serve as powerful responses to mainstream society, prompting a reevaluation of what it means to live authentically and pursue happiness in a world that often imposes restrictive identities.

As we reflect on these historical examples of ethical resistance, we are reminded of the profound potential within each of us to effect change. The stories of those who dared to dissent teach us that mindfulness and intentional action can influence political engagement and contribute to a reimagined democracy. By embracing unconventional philosophies and acknowledging our inner drive for a more fulfilling life, we can cultivate a society that honors the dignity of every individual. In doing so, we not only honor the legacy of those who came before us but also pave the way for future generations to continue the vital work of justice and social transformation.

MINDFULNESS AND POLITICAL ENGAGEMENT

The Role of Awareness in Activism

Awareness serves as the cornerstone of effective activism, illuminating the path toward meaningful social change. In a world often clouded by misinformation and apathy, the ability to recognize injustices and understand their roots is crucial. This heightened awareness empowers individuals to transcend passive existence, igniting a passion for action that challenges the status quo. By cultivating a deep understanding of societal structures and their impact on human lives, activists can articulate their grievances and aspirations more clearly, fostering a collective consciousness that is essential for any movement striving for progress.

In the context of individual agency, awareness acts as a catalyst for personal empowerment. Recognizing one's ability to influence change transforms individuals from mere observers to active participants in shaping their communities. This shift emboldens people to question existing norms and challenge oppressive systems that stifle their potential. As individuals become more attuned to their surroundings, they often find the courage to embrace non-conformity, which is a vital aspect of political activism. The act of stepping outside conventional boundaries not only inspires others but also invites innovative solutions to age-old problems, creating a ripple effect that can lead to systemic transformation.

The intersection of existentialism and political activism further underscores the importance of awareness in fostering social change. When individuals confront the inherent absurdity of life, they often discover a profound sense of responsibility toward their fellow beings. This realization can catalyze a commitment to activism, as people seek to create meaning in a world that often feels chaotic. By embracing their freedom and understanding the weight of their choices, activists can cultivate a sense of purpose that drives their efforts. This philosophical grounding allows them to navigate the complexities of social movements with resilience and creativity, ensuring that their actions resonate on both personal and collective levels.

Moreover, the philosophy of happiness intertwines with social justice, illustrating that awareness of societal inequities is essential for fostering genuine fulfillment. As individuals recognize the interconnectedness of their well-being with the welfare of their communities, they often feel compelled to advocate for systemic change. This understanding cultivates a sense of solidarity, as personal joy becomes inextricably linked to the struggles of others. By prioritizing collective happiness and advocating for inclusive policies, activists can reimagine democracy in a way that honors the dignity and aspirations of all individuals, fostering a society rooted in empathy and justice.

Ultimately, mindfulness plays a pivotal role in enhancing political engagement by sharpening awareness and fostering a deeper connection to the present moment. When individuals practice mindfulness, they become more attuned to the nuances of their experiences, allowing them to respond to societal issues with clarity and intentionality. This heightened awareness not only enriches personal fulfillment but also strengthens community well-being. By cultivating a mindful approach to activism, individuals can navigate the complexities of social change with grace, ensuring that their actions resonate with authenticity and purpose. In this reimagined landscape of democracy, awareness emerges as a powerful force, illuminating the path toward a more equitable and fulfilling society for all.

PRACTICES FOR MINDFUL POLITICAL INVOLVEMENT

Practices for mindful political involvement invite individuals to engage deeply with the complexities of democracy while remaining grounded in their personal values and experiences. This approach encourages adults to view political engagement not merely as a duty but as an opportunity for personal growth and societal transformation. By cultivating mindfulness, individuals can navigate the often chaotic political landscape with clarity and intention, fostering a deeper connection to both themselves and the communities they serve.

Mindful political involvement begins with self-reflection, enabling individuals to understand their beliefs, biases, and motivations. This inner exploration is crucial for recognizing how personal experiences shape one's political perspective. By taking the time to examine our values and the influences that have shaped them, we can participate in political discussions authentically and empathetically. This self-awareness not only enriches our understanding but also enhances our ability to listen to others, creating a more inclusive dialogue that respects diverse viewpoints.

Another vital practice is the cultivation of presence in our political activities. Whether attending town hall meetings, engaging in grassroots organizing, or participating in protests, being fully present allows us to absorb the nuances of each situation. This presence fosters a deeper connection to the issues at hand and the individuals involved. It helps us to respond thoughtfully rather than react impulsively, transforming our political actions into meaningful contributions rather than mere reactions to external stimuli.

Moreover, integrating mindfulness into political involvement encourages a holistic view of activism that recognizes the interdependence of personal fulfillment and community well-being. By prioritizing self-care and personal development, individuals can sustain their energy and passion for social change. This balance is essential in combating burnout and disillusionment, common pitfalls in the realm of activism. When we commit to our own growth, we are better equipped to contribute to a larger movement, creating a ripple effect that enhances the collective effort toward justice and equity.

Finally, embracing an ethical framework for dissent and civil disobedience rooted in mindfulness can empower individuals to challenge oppressive systems without losing sight of their inner values. This approach allows for dissent to be viewed as a constructive force—an expression of love for humanity and a commitment to social justice. By engaging in mindful political practices, we not only advocate for change but also embody the very principles of compassion, understanding, and community that are essential for a thriving democracy. In this way, we reimagine political engagement as a transformative process, one that nurtures both the individual spirit and the collective heart of society.

PERSONAL FULFILLMENT AND COMMUNITY WELLBEING

The Interconnection of Individual and Collective Health

The interconnection of individual and collective health represents a profound tapestry woven from the threads of personal well-being and societal flourishing. As we navigate the complexities of modern life, it becomes increasingly clear that the health of an individual is inextricably linked to the health of the community. This relationship challenges the conventional dichotomy between self-interest and collective good, inviting us to recognize that our personal journeys toward fulfillment can catalyze broader social change. By embracing the idea that individual agency fuels collective movements, we unlock the potential for transformative action that resonates deeply within the fabric of society.

At the heart of this interconnection lies the understanding that personal well-being transcends mere physical health. It encompasses emotional resilience, mental clarity, and a sense of purpose. When individuals cultivate these attributes, they not only enhance their own lives but also contribute to the vitality of their communities. This reciprocal relationship is particularly evident in social movements, where the collective strength of individuals united by a shared vision can lead to profound societal shifts. Each act of dissent, rooted in personal conviction, reverberates through the collective consciousness, inspiring others and fostering a sense of solidarity that can challenge oppressive systems.

Non-conformity plays a pivotal role in this dynamic, serving as a catalyst for change and innovation. Individuals who dare to step outside societal norms often illuminate paths others may not see, encouraging a reevaluation of entrenched beliefs and practices. This spirit of rebellion, when rooted in a quest for personal fulfillment, transforms into a collective call for justice and equality. As we embrace alternative lifestyles and unconventional philosophies, we begin to unravel the rigid structures of mainstream society, crafting a narrative that prioritizes well-being and fulfillment for all, rather than a select few.

Existentialism further enriches this discourse, positing that individual freedom and responsibility are essential in the pursuit of a just society. It compels us to confront the existential dilemmas faced by individuals within oppressive systems, urging a commitment to activism that is both personally meaningful and socially impactful. By recognizing our interconnectedness, we can engage in mindfulness practices that enhance our political engagement, grounding our activism in a deeper understanding of ourselves and our shared humanity. In this way, the quest for personal happiness aligns seamlessly with the pursuit of social justice, reinforcing the notion that our individual journeys are integral to the collective narrative.

Ultimately, reimagining democracy through unconventional perspectives calls for a radical embrace of the interconnectedness of individual and collective health. By prioritizing personal fulfillment as a cornerstone of societal well-being, we pave the way for a more empathetic and just world. This vision encourages us to challenge the status quo, engage in civil disobedience when necessary, and advocate for ethical practices that honor both individual and communal needs. In doing so, we not only reclaim our agency but also elevate the health of our society, creating a vibrant dialogue that honors the complexity of human experience and the transformative power of collective action.

STRATEGIES FOR CULTIVATING COMMUNITY CONNECTIONS

Cultivating community connections is a vital strategy for fostering a sense of belonging and engagement in a world that often feels fragmented. At the heart of this endeavor lies the recognition that each individual possesses unique strengths and perspectives that can contribute to a richer communal tapestry. By embracing the philosophy of interconnectedness, individuals can initiate meaningful dialogues that transcend conventional boundaries. Encouraging open discussions about shared values and aspirations allows communities to build a foundation based on trust, mutual respect, and the recognition of our shared humanity. This process not only enriches personal lives but also strengthens the collective resolve to pursue social change.

One effective way to cultivate these connections is through grassroots initiatives that bring people together around common interests or goals. Organizing local events such as workshops, art exhibitions, or community gardens can serve as catalysts for interaction and collaboration. These platforms allow diverse voices to be heard and foster a spirit of inclusivity, enabling individuals from various backgrounds to engage in co-creation. Such initiatives not only promote social cohesion but also empower participants to take ownership of their community's future, reinforcing the idea that each person has a vital role to play in shaping the collective narrative.

Another powerful strategy is to harness the potential of storytelling as a means of connection. Sharing personal experiences of struggle and triumph can evoke empathy and understanding, bridging the gaps between different life experiences. Storytelling creates a safe space for vulnerability and encourages individuals to reflect on their own journeys while appreciating the complexities of others. This practice aligns closely with existentialist principles, as it encourages individuals to confront their own realities while recognizing the interconnectedness of their existence with those around them. By fostering a culture of openness and authenticity, communities can cultivate deeper connections that inspire collective action.

Mindfulness practices can also play a crucial role in enhancing community connections. By promoting self-awareness and emotional intelligence, mindfulness encourages individuals to engage with others from a place of compassion and empathy. When people learn to listen actively and respond thoughtfully, the quality of interactions improves, leading to more profound relationships. This mindful approach can be particularly transformative in political activism, where heated emotions often cloud rational discourse. By grounding oneself in the present moment, individuals can better navigate conflicts and foster a spirit of cooperation, ultimately driving social change from a place of understanding rather than division.

Finally, reimagining democracy through unconventional perspectives requires a commitment to nurturing connections at all levels. Individuals must recognize the power of their agency in shaping the world around them and engage in dialogues that challenge mainstream narratives. By embracing alternative lifestyles and philosophies, individuals can inspire others to rethink their roles within the community and the broader political landscape. This shift in consciousness can lead to a flourishing of diverse ideas and practices that not only enhance personal fulfillment but also contribute to the well-being of the community as a whole. Ultimately, cultivating community connections is not just a strategy for social change; it is an essential element of living a more fulfilling and harmonious life in a society that often overlooks the profound interconnectedness of our shared human experience.

INNOVATIVE APPROACHES TO CIVIC ENGAGEMENT

Innovative approaches to civic engagement are essential in a world where traditional methods often fail to resonate with the evolving aspirations of individuals. As people seek deeper connections to their communities and a more profound sense of purpose, it becomes clear that civic engagement must transcend conventional boundaries. By embracing innovative strategies that tap into the core of human experience, we can foster a culture of active participation that inspires individuals to reclaim their agency and contribute meaningfully to society.

One such approach is the integration of mindfulness into civic practices. Mindfulness encourages individuals to cultivate awareness and presence, enabling them to engage with political issues not merely as detached observers but as active participants.

This shift in perspective can transform how individuals relate to their communities and the political landscape, fostering a sense of responsibility and empowerment. By recognizing their thoughts, emotions, and actions, individuals can approach civic engagement with clarity and intention, inspiring others to follow suit and create a ripple effect of meaningful involvement.

Another innovative method involves harnessing the power of technology to create platforms for dialogue and collaboration. Digital tools can facilitate connections among diverse voices, allowing for the exchange of ideas that challenge the status quo. This democratization of information empowers individuals to share their experiences and perspectives, breaking down silos that often isolate communities. As people engage in these online spaces, they can cultivate a collective identity rooted in shared values and aspirations, thereby redefining the landscape of civic engagement and social change.

Moreover, the intersection of art and activism presents a vibrant avenue for innovative civic engagement. Artistic expression has the power to evoke emotions, challenge perceptions, and inspire action. By utilizing creative mediums, individuals can communicate their visions for a more just and equitable society in ways that resonate deeply with others. This engagement not only enriches the cultural fabric of communities but also activates a broader discourse on social issues, inviting participation from those who may otherwise feel alienated from traditional political mechanisms.

Finally, the cultivation of alternative lifestyles as a form of civic engagement encourages individuals to live out their values authentically. By opting for sustainable practices, cooperative living arrangements, or community-driven initiatives, people can embody their beliefs and challenge the prevailing narratives of mainstream society. These choices reflect a commitment to personal fulfillment and collective well-being, illustrating that civic engagement is not limited to formal political participation but can manifest in everyday actions. In this way, innovative approaches to civic engagement empower individuals to reimagine democracy and create a world that aligns more closely with the innate desires of humanity.

EXISTENTIALISM AND PERSONAL RESPONSIBILITY

Existentialism places a profound emphasis on personal responsibility, urging individuals to confront their freedom and the weight of their choices. In a world increasingly dominated by authoritarian regimes and oligarchic power structures, this philosophical perspective empowers citizens to reclaim their agency. The essence of existentialist thought lies in the belief that every choice we make shapes not only our own lives but also the collective fate of our societies. As we navigate the complexities of modern governance, the call for personal responsibility becomes not just a moral imperative but a revolutionary act against the tides of oppression.

In democratic participation, the existentialist perspective challenges individuals to engage deeply with their political environment. It encourages a critical examination of one's values and beliefs, pushing each person to question the status quo and the systems that govern them. This engagement is not merely about casting a vote; it is about understanding the implications of one's choices and recognizing the interconnectedness of personal actions and societal outcomes. By embracing personal responsibility, individuals can become catalysts for change, fostering a culture of accountability that resists the allure of authoritarianism.

Furthermore, existentialism invites us to confront the often uncomfortable truths of our existence, including the realities of inequality and injustice. In the face of systemic oppression, acknowledging our responsibility can be a source of empowerment. This recognition compels us to challenge the narratives that uphold existing power structures, urging us to envision a more inclusive and equitable form of governance. Engaging with existentialist thought inspires a commitment to social change that transcends mere compliance, driving individuals to advocate for the rights and dignity of all members of society.

As we explore the intersections of eco-philosophy and sustainable governance, the existential call to personal responsibility becomes even more relevant. In an era marked by environmental degradation and climate crisis, understanding our role in shaping a sustainable future is crucial. By adopting an existentialist framework, we can see our choices—whether they relate to consumption, political engagement, or community involvement—as powerful tools for enacting change. This perspective not only emphasizes the urgency of environmental ethics but also encourages a collective responsibility that recognizes our shared humanity and the planet we inhabit.

In reimagining democracy, we must embrace the existentialist challenge to take ownership of our political engagement. By cultivating a mindset that values personal responsibility, we can foster a robust resistance to authoritarianism and envision a future that is not only just but also sustainable. This journey requires courage and commitment, as it calls on each of us to confront our own complicity in systems of power. Ultimately, the existentialist perspective offers a pathway toward a more engaged and ethical citizenry, empowering individuals to transform their lives and the world around them in meaningful ways.

RETHINKING GOVERNANCE THROUGH DIVERSE NARRATIVES

Rethinking governance through diverse narratives invites us to challenge the entrenched paradigms that currently define our political systems. In a world increasingly characterized by authoritarianism and oligarchic structures, the need for a new vision of democracy becomes ever more pressing. By embracing a multitude of perspectives—rooted in existentialism, eco-philosophy, feminist political theory, and post-colonial thought—we can craft a governance model that reflects the complexity of human experience and acknowledges the historical injustices that have shaped our societies. This is not merely an academic exercise; it is a call to action for individuals to engage deeply with the narratives that inform their political beliefs and practices.

Existentialism emphasizes the importance of personal responsibility and authentic engagement in the democratic process. In this light, each individual must confront their role within a flawed system and recognize the power of their voice in shaping collective outcomes. As we stand firm against the encroachment of authoritarianism, it is essential to cultivate a sense of agency that inspires active participation. By embracing our responsibility, we can foster a political culture that prioritizes ethical leadership and challenges the status quo, transforming passive acceptance into dynamic engagement.

Eco-philosophy further enriches our understanding of governance by integrating environmental ethics into the political discourse. In an age where climate change threatens the very fabric of our existence, reimagining democracy through the lens of sustainability is imperative. This perspective compels us to consider the interconnectedness of human rights and ecological health, advocating for policies that prioritize both the planet and its inhabitants. By envisioning a governance model that respects environmental limits, we can cultivate a society that values long-term ecological stewardship over short-term gains, thus ensuring a more equitable future for generations to come.

Feminist political theory challenges traditional power structures by emphasizing inclusivity and diversity in governance. By rethinking authority through a feminist lens, we can dismantle hierarchical systems that perpetuate oppression and inequality. This approach not only advocates for the representation of marginalized voices but also encourages a participatory model of governance that values collaboration and consensus. Embracing feminist principles allows us to envision a more just political landscape where the rights and experiences of all individuals are recognized and respected.

Finally, the influence of technology on democracy cannot be overlooked. As digital platforms reshape political engagement, we must critically analyze their role in reinforcing or dismantling power dynamics. The potential for grassroots movements to flourish in the digital age presents an opportunity to explore anarchist principles of non-hierarchical governance. By harnessing the power of technology for social change, we can forge connections that transcend traditional boundaries, fostering a collective vision for a more equitable society. In this reimagined landscape, diverse narratives become not just a source of inspiration but a vital foundation for a democracy that truly reflects the will and needs of its people.

BUILDING EQUITABLE POLITICAL SYSTEMS

Building equitable political systems requires a profound commitment to reimagining democracy through the lens of diverse philosophical perspectives. In an age where authoritarianism often masquerades as stability, it is imperative that we embrace unconventional philosophies that champion social change. This means actively engaging with ideas that challenge traditional structures and advocate for a more inclusive and representative governance model. By intertwining existentialism with political engagement, we recognize our personal responsibility in shaping democratic participation, ensuring that every voice is heard and valued in the political arena.

Feminist political theory plays a pivotal role in dismantling entrenched power dynamics that have historically marginalized voices. By advocating for gender equity and inclusivity, we can craft political systems that genuinely reflect the diverse experiences and needs of the population. This approach not only enriches democratic discourse but also fosters a sense of belonging among those who have been systematically excluded. In embracing feminist principles, we recognize that true democracy cannot thrive without the empowerment of all individuals, particularly those who have faced oppression due to their gender, race, or socio-economic status.

Post-colonial perspectives further enhance our understanding of democracy by highlighting the historical injustices that continue to shape contemporary political landscapes. By acknowledging the lingering effects of colonialism, we can begin to deconstruct the power structures that perpetuate inequality and disenfranchisement. This critical examination allows us to envision a political system that is not only equitable but also restorative, addressing past wrongs while fostering a more just future. In this context, building equitable political systems requires a commitment to reparative justice and an acknowledgment of the diverse narratives that inform our shared history.

The impact of technology on democracy cannot be overlooked in our quest for equitable governance. Digital platforms have transformed the way we engage with politics, offering new avenues for participation and expression. However, they also pose significant challenges, such as the risk of misinformation and the monopolization of power by a select few. To build equitable political systems, we must advocate for transparent and inclusive digital spaces that empower citizens rather than silence them. This entails harnessing technology as a tool for democratic engagement, ensuring that it serves the interests of the many rather than the privileged few.

Ultimately, the role of ethics in political leadership is crucial in the fight against authoritarianism and the preservation of human rights. Leaders must embody moral responsibility, not only in their policies but also in their actions and decisions. By fostering an ethical political culture, we can cultivate trust and accountability, essential components for sustainable governance. As we navigate the complexities of modern politics, let us remain steadfast in our pursuit of equitable systems that honor the dignity of every individual and promote a thriving, participatory democracy for generations to come.

ECO-PHILOSOPHY AND SUSTAINABLE GOVERNANCE

Environmental Ethics in Political Decision-Making

Environmental ethics plays a crucial role in political decision-making, especially in an age where the consequences of climate change and ecosystem degradation are profoundly felt. It urges leaders to prioritize the health of the planet alongside the needs of their constituents, fostering a moral responsibility that transcends traditional political agendas. By integrating environmental considerations into the fabric of governance, we can cultivate a political landscape that not only addresses immediate human concerns but also safeguards the ecological systems that sustain life. This holistic approach challenges the short-sightedness often seen in authoritarian regimes, which prioritize power and profit over the well-being of their citizens and the environment.

As we reimagine democracy, embracing unconventional philosophies can ignite a transformative vision for governance. Environmental ethics can serve as a foundational principle for inclusive decision-making, ensuring that marginalized voices—particularly those of indigenous communities and future generations—are heard. This inclusivity is vital in dismantling oppressive structures, as it acknowledges the interconnectedness of social justice and ecological sustainability. By framing environmental issues as ethical dilemmas, political leaders can foster a sense of collective responsibility, encouraging citizens to engage actively with their government and advocate for policies that promote ecological integrity.

In the context of existentialism and political engagement, the emphasis on personal responsibility becomes paramount. Each individual has the capacity to influence political discourse and action, particularly regarding environmental issues. This understanding empowers citizens to hold their leaders accountable, demanding that policies reflect ethical considerations for the environment. By cultivating a culture of responsibility, we can inspire a generation of activists who view political participation as a moral obligation, thus creating a robust democratic framework that resists authoritarianism and nurtures ecological stewardship.

The intersection of feminist political theory and environmental ethics reveals the need for diverse perspectives in shaping sustainable governance. Traditional power structures often neglect the voices of women and marginalized groups, who are disproportionately affected by environmental degradation. By challenging these norms, feminist approaches can illuminate the importance of inclusive governance that integrates environmental concerns with social equity. This synergy not only enhances democratic participation but also fosters innovative solutions to pressing ecological challenges, creating a more resilient and just society.

Finally, as we navigate a world increasingly influenced by technology, the integration of environmental ethics into political decision-making becomes even more critical. Digital platforms can facilitate greater engagement and awareness around ecological issues, empowering citizens to advocate for sustainable policies. However, these same technologies can also amplify authoritarian tendencies if misused. By grounding our political engagement in ethical principles, we can harness the power of technology to promote transparency, accountability, and ecological consciousness, ensuring that the future of democracy is rooted in a commitment to both human rights and environmental sustainability.

RETHINKING DEMOCRACY THROUGH ECO-CENTRIC POLICIES

Rethinking democracy through eco-centric policies invites us to embrace a transformative vision that harmonizes our political structures with the natural world. This approach recognizes that the health of our planet is intrinsically linked to the health of our societies. By prioritizing ecological sustainability in governance, we create a framework that not only addresses environmental crises but also promotes social equity and justice. This reimagining of democracy demands that we reject oppressive systems that prioritize profit over people and the planet, and instead embrace policies that foster a deep respect for all forms of life. In doing so, we empower communities to reclaim their agency, ensuring that the voices of the marginalized are amplified in decision-making processes.

An eco-centric democracy emphasizes the importance of integrating environmental ethics into our political discourse. This means recognizing the rights of nature alongside human rights, and understanding that our survival is intertwined with the ecosystems that sustain us. Such a perspective calls for a radical shift away from anthropocentrism, challenging traditional power structures that have long marginalized ecological considerations. By fostering a political environment where ecological wisdom is prioritized, we can build resilient societies capable of facing the challenges posed by climate change and environmental degradation. This reorientation towards eco-centric policies serves as a powerful antidote to the authoritarian tendencies that arise from resource scarcity and environmental collapse.

The engagement of citizens in eco-centric policies is not merely a matter of environmental advocacy; it represents a profound existential responsibility. Each individual has a role to play in shaping the democratic landscape, advocating for sustainable practices that reflect our interconnectedness with the earth. This participatory approach encourages grassroots movements, empowering citizens to challenge the status quo and demand accountability from their leaders. By fostering a sense of collective responsibility, we cultivate a culture of activism that transcends individual interests, ultimately leading to a more inclusive and equitable democratic process.

Feminist political theory plays a crucial role in this reimagining of democracy by challenging traditional power dynamics that perpetuate inequalities. An eco-centric framework aligns with feminist principles, advocating for an inclusive governance model that recognizes the contributions of all individuals, particularly those historically marginalized. By integrating feminist perspectives into eco-centric policies, we create a more holistic approach to governance that addresses the intersections of gender, race, and environmental justice. This synthesis not only enriches our democratic ideals but also paves the way for innovative solutions to the pressing challenges we face as a society.

Ultimately, rethinking democracy through eco-centric policies inspires a vision of governance that is as diverse and dynamic as the ecosystems we inhabit. By embracing alternative philosophies that prioritize sustainability, social justice, and collective well-being, we can forge a path towards a more just and equitable society. This journey requires courage and commitment, as we challenge entrenched systems of power and demand a political landscape that reflects our deepest values. In standing firm against authoritarianism and advocating for eco-centric policies, we not only safeguard our planet but also affirm the dignity and rights of all its inhabitants, embodying the very essence of a true democracy.

THE INTERSECTION OF ECOLOGY AND SOCIAL JUSTICE

The intersection of ecology and social justice represents a pivotal space for reimagining democracy amidst the challenges of authoritarianism and oligarchic systems. In today's political landscape, the environmental crisis disproportionately affects marginalized communities, revealing the urgent need to link ecological sustainability with social equity. This connection urges us to rethink governance structures and advocate for policies that prioritize the voices of those historically silenced. By recognizing that the health of our planet is intrinsically tied to the well-being of its inhabitants, we can cultivate a more inclusive and ethical approach to leadership that embraces the principles of justice and environmental stewardship.

Embracing eco-philosophy within the framework of social justice compels us to confront the oppressive systems that perpetuate inequality. The exploitation of natural resources is often mirrored by the exploitation of marginalized groups. As we engage in political discourse, it is essential to challenge traditional power structures that prioritize profit over people and the planet. This requires a concerted effort to elevate grassroots movements that advocate for sustainable practices and equitable resource distribution. By fostering a culture of solidarity, we can dismantle the barriers erected by authoritarian regimes and create a political environment where every voice contributes to the collective vision of a just society.

Existentialism plays a crucial role in our understanding of personal responsibility within democratic participation. Each individual must confront their role in the broader ecological and social landscape, recognizing that their actions impact both the environment and their community. This awareness fosters a sense of agency and inspires citizens to engage actively in the political process. By embracing our responsibilities, we can collectively challenge the status quo, advocating for policies that uphold human rights and environmental integrity. This moral engagement is essential in resisting the allure of authoritarianism, which often thrives on apathy and disconnection from community values.

Feminist political theory further enriches the dialogue at this intersection by challenging conventional notions of power and governance. By integrating feminist perspectives, we can envision a political framework that is not only equitable but also deeply attuned to the complexities of human relationships and ecological interdependence. This approach advocates for the inclusion of diverse voices in decision-making processes, ensuring that policies reflect the needs of all societal members, particularly those who have been historically marginalized. The reimagining of governance through this lens can lead to transformative changes that promote social justice while fostering environmental sustainability.

In an era where technology shapes our political engagement, we must remain vigilant about its implications for both ecology and social justice. Digital platforms can serve as powerful tools for grassroots activism and community organizing, enabling marginalized groups to amplify their voices and advocate for change. However, the potential for surveillance and control also looms large. As we navigate this landscape, it is vital to maintain a critical perspective on how technology influences power dynamics within society. By harnessing the potential of digital tools while remaining aware of their limitations, we can forge a path toward a more just and sustainable democracy that honors the intricate relationship between ecological health and social equity.

FEMINIST POLITICAL THEORY
Challenging Traditional Power Structures

Challenging traditional power structures requires a profound re-examination of our political landscapes, urging us to question the legitimacy of long-standing hierarchies that often perpetuate inequality and oppression. In a world where authoritarianism and oligarchy threaten the very essence of democracy, it becomes imperative to explore unconventional philosophies that advocate for radical change. This entails not only a critique of existing power dynamics but also an embrace of diverse perspectives that emphasize inclusivity, responsibility, and sustainability. By interrogating the foundations of these structures, we can begin to envision a more equitable society that prioritizes the voices and rights of all individuals.

At the heart of this challenge lies the philosophical underpinnings of existentialism, which calls for personal responsibility in democratic participation. Each individual must confront the reality of their agency in the face of systemic injustices and recognize that their choices can either uphold or dismantle oppressive structures. This existential engagement invites us to actively participate in shaping our political realities, rejecting complacency, and instead fostering a culture of accountability and ethical leadership. Embracing this perspective not only empowers individuals to take a stand against tyranny but also cultivates a collective consciousness that prioritizes moral integrity in governance.

Furthermore, eco-philosophy offers a vital lens through which we can rethink democracy, emphasizing the interconnection between environmental stewardship and social justice. As the planet faces unprecedented ecological crises, the need for sustainable governance becomes paramount. This approach challenges traditional power structures by advocating for a political system that prioritizes the well-being of the planet and its inhabitants. By integrating environmental ethics into our democratic practices, we can foster a new paradigm that respects the rights of nature while promoting a holistic vision of justice that transcends anthropocentric boundaries.

Feminist political theory also plays a crucial role in dismantling entrenched power hierarchies. By critiquing patriarchal structures and advocating for inclusive governance, feminist thought encourages the reimagining of political systems that reflect the diverse experiences and needs of marginalized groups. This approach not only enriches our understanding of democracy but also underscores the necessity of intersectionality in political discourse. As we challenge traditional notions of authority, we can pave the way for a more just and inclusive society where all voices are heard and valued.

In an age where technology permeates every aspect of our lives, it is essential to analyze its impact on political engagement and power dynamics. Digital platforms have the potential to democratize information and empower grassroots movements, yet they can also reinforce existing inequalities. By critically examining the role of technology in shaping our political landscape, we can explore innovative ways to enhance democratic participation and challenge oppressive systems. This multifaceted approach encourages us to envision a future where power is decentralized, and communities are empowered to govern

themselves in ways that reflect their unique values and aspirations. Through these explorations, we can collectively forge a path toward a more just and equitable society, rooted in ethical leadership and a commitment to challenging traditional power structures.

INCLUSIVE GOVERNANCE AND REPRESENTATION

Inclusive governance and representation stand as pillars in the quest for a truly democratic society, where every voice is valued and every individual has a stake in the decision-making processes that govern their lives. In a world increasingly marked by authoritarian tendencies and oligarchic structures, the call for a political system that embraces diversity and inclusivity grows ever more urgent. This challenge invites us to reimagine democracy not merely as a procedural framework but as a living ethos that reflects the complexity of human experiences. By fostering inclusive governance, we can create spaces where marginalized voices are amplified, thereby enriching the democratic dialogue and ensuring that policies reflect the needs of all citizens.

The philosophical underpinnings of inclusive governance draw heavily from feminist political theory and post-colonial perspectives, which challenge traditional power structures that have long sidelined diverse identities. By acknowledging historical injustices and the systemic barriers faced by various communities, we can begin to dismantle the hegemony of dominant narratives in governance. This reimagining of democratic processes demands a commitment to listening actively, engaging empathetically, and understanding the unique challenges faced by different groups. Through this lens, we can envision a political landscape where inclusivity is not an afterthought but the foundation upon which our governance is built.

Moreover, the intertwining of eco-philosophy and sustainable governance presents a compelling argument for inclusive representation. As we confront the environmental crises of our time, it becomes imperative that governance reflects the voices of those most affected by ecological degradation, often the marginalized and disenfranchised. Inclusive governance recognizes the interconnectedness of social justice and environmental stewardship, advocating for a model of democracy that prioritizes the voices of indigenous peoples, local communities, and those who have historically been ignored. By placing environmental ethics at the forefront of our political engagement, we can cultivate a more sustainable and just society.

The role of technology in shaping political engagement cannot be overlooked in this discourse. Digital platforms offer unprecedented opportunities for grassroots movements to flourish, challenging traditional hierarchies and promoting non-hierarchical systems of governance. However, this potential is coupled with the risks of surveillance, misinformation, and the centralization of power in the hands of a few. To harness technology as a tool for inclusive governance, we must advocate for transparent digital practices that empower citizens rather than subjugate them. This critical engagement with technology can help redefine the terms of political participation, ensuring that the democratic process is accessible to all.

Finally, the relationship between ethics and political leadership is crucial in the pursuit of inclusive governance. As moral leaders, we are called to uphold the principles of justice, equity, and accountability in the face of authoritarianism. This commitment to ethical governance requires a deep introspection into our individual roles in the democratic process. By embracing a philosophy of rights that respects and protects the dignity of every individual, we can foster a culture of participation that not only challenges oppressive systems but also inspires collective action toward a more inclusive future. In this endeavor, each of us bears the responsibility to engage critically, act courageously, and advocate passionately for a democracy that truly reflects the richness of human experience.

THE ROLE OF GENDER IN POLITICAL ENGAGEMENT

The intersection of gender and political engagement reveals profound insights into how power structures evolve and how they can be challenged. Gender roles have historically dictated the terms of political participation, often marginalizing voices that challenge conventional authority. Women and gender minorities have long been at the forefront of social movements, embodying a resistance that calls for not just inclusion but a fundamental reshaping of governance itself. By examining the role of gender in political engagement, we can uncover pathways to a more equitable and just democracy that embraces diverse perspectives and experiences.

Feminist political theory serves as a critical lens through which to understand the dynamics of power and authority. It challenges traditional structures by advocating for a political framework that recognizes the contributions and rights of all genders. This reimagining fosters an environment where moral leadership is not only defined by authority but by the ability to inspire and mobilize communities. As we witness the rise of grassroots movements led by women and marginalized genders, it becomes evident that their involvement is essential for dismantling oppressive systems and promoting inclusive governance that reflects the values of a diverse citizenry.

Furthermore, the integration of gender perspectives into political engagement is not merely about representation; it is about reshaping the very fabric of decision-making processes. When women and gender minorities engage in politics, they bring unique insights that can lead to more holistic and sustainable policies. This engagement fosters a deeper understanding of the interconnectedness of social justice, environmental sustainability, and human rights. By prioritizing gender equity in political discourse, we can initiate a paradigm shift that recognizes the ethical implications of governance and promotes a collective responsibility for the well-being of all.

In exploring existentialism in political participation, we confront the notion of personal responsibility. Each individual, regardless of gender, has a role to play in shaping the political landscape. This engagement is not only an expression of rights but a moral obligation to challenge injustices and advocate for change. The courage to stand firm against authoritarianism and to resist the encroachment on human rights is a shared responsibility that transcends gender. By fostering a culture of active engagement, we empower individuals to embrace their agency and redefine their roles within the political sphere.

Ultimately, the role of gender in political engagement is a powerful force for reimagining democracy. As we navigate the complexities of contemporary governance, we must champion diverse voices that challenge the status quo and advocate for ethical leadership. This journey towards a more inclusive democracy requires us to confront our biases, embrace unconventional philosophies, and recognize the potential for transformative social change. By doing so, we lay the groundwork for a future where every individual, regardless of gender, contributes to a political landscape that values justice, equity, and the flourishing of humanity.

ANARCHISM AND ALTERNATIVE GOVERNANCE

Grassroots Movements and Social Change

Grassroots movements have emerged as powerful forces for social change, rooted in the belief that collective action can dismantle oppressive structures and foster a more equitable society. These movements often arise from local communities, motivated by shared experiences of injustice and a desire for transformation. They embody a fundamental principle of democracy: that power should originate from the people and reflect their will. By organizing at the grassroots level, individuals reclaim their agency and challenge the status quo, inspiring others to join in a shared vision for a better future. This reimagining of democracy not only empowers participants but also serves as a beacon of hope for those living under authoritarian regimes or oligarchic systems.

The philosophical underpinnings of grassroots movements draw heavily from existentialism, emphasizing personal responsibility and the importance of individual engagement in the democratic process. Each participant in a grassroots initiative is not merely a follower; rather, they are active agents of change, confronting their fears and doubts to stand firm against oppressive forces. This personal commitment to democratic ideals fosters a sense of ownership and accountability, vital for sustaining momentum in the fight for justice. As individuals recognize their collective power, they become catalysts for broader societal transformation, challenging existing power dynamics and advocating for rights that have been historically marginalized.

Eco-philosophy offers a critical lens through which to view grassroots movements, particularly in relation to sustainable governance. Environmental degradation and social injustice are often intertwined, and grassroots initiatives frequently address both issues simultaneously. By advocating for eco-friendly practices and policies, these movements highlight the ethical imperative of caring for our planet while ensuring that all voices are heard in the decision-making process. This intersection of environmental and social justice not only redefines the parameters of democracy but also emphasizes the importance of inclusivity in governance—an essential aspect of fostering resilience in the face of systemic challenges.

Feminist political theory further enriches the discourse on grassroots movements by challenging traditional power structures and advocating for a more inclusive approach to governance. Feminist activists have historically been at the forefront of grassroots efforts, using their voices to expose injustices and advocate for equity across all spheres of life. By centering marginalized perspectives, these movements push for a reimagining of political systems that prioritizes the needs and rights of the most vulnerable. This inclusive governance model not only strengthens democratic engagement but also fosters a sense of belonging and agency among all participants, paving the way for significant societal change.

In the age of technology, grassroots movements are increasingly leveraging digital platforms to amplify their messages and organize efforts. This technological engagement has transformed the landscape of political participation, allowing individuals to connect across vast distances and mobilize quickly in response to injustices. However, it also raises critical questions about power dynamics and the potential for surveillance and control. Navigating these complexities requires a commitment to ethical leadership and a dedication to safeguarding human rights. Ultimately, grassroots movements embody the spirit of resistance against authoritarianism, demonstrating that even in the face of overwhelming odds, collective action can pave the way for a more just and equitable society.

NON-HIERARCHICAL SYSTEMS OF ORGANIZATION

Non-hierarchical systems of organization present a transformative vision for governance, one that disrupts the entrenched structures of authority that often stifle creativity, collaboration, and true democratic engagement. In a world where authoritarianism and oligarchy threaten the very fabric of our societies, these systems invite us to reimagine our political landscapes. By promoting decentralized decision-making and empowering individuals at the grassroots level, non-hierarchical organizations embody a radical departure from traditional power dynamics, challenging us to envision a future grounded in justice, equality, and shared responsibility.

At the heart of non-hierarchical systems lies the principle of collective autonomy, which fosters an environment where every voice is not only heard but valued. This approach is particularly resonant in the context of existentialist thought, which emphasizes individual agency and the importance of personal responsibility in shaping our collective fate. By engaging in democratic participation that eschews rigid hierarchies, individuals can take ownership of their roles in society, actively contributing to the shaping of policies and practices that affect their lives. This empowerment can lead to profound personal transformations, encouraging individuals not only to stand firm against authoritarian regimes but also to cultivate a sense of community and solidarity.

Eco-philosophy further enriches the discourse around non-hierarchical systems by advocating for governance structures that prioritize environmental sustainability and social equity. In recognizing the interconnectedness of humanity and the planet, these systems challenge us to redefine our relationship with nature and with one another. By integrating ecological ethics into our political frameworks, we can foster a governance model that is responsive to the urgent challenges of climate change and resource depletion, ensuring that future generations inherit a world that is not only livable but thriving. This holistic perspective reaffirms the necessity of inclusive governance, one that transcends traditional boundaries and embraces diverse voices, particularly those historically marginalized in political discourse.

Feminist political theory adds another critical layer to the conversation on non-hierarchical organization. It calls for the dismantling of patriarchal structures that perpetuate inequality and exclusion. By advocating for collaborative leadership and shared decision-making, feminist frameworks challenge us to envision a governance model that reflects the diverse experiences and needs of all citizens. This inclusive approach not only enriches democratic participation but also empowers individuals to engage actively in shaping policies that impact their lives, fostering a culture of accountability and mutual respect that is essential for any healthy democracy.

As technology continues to reshape our political landscape, non-hierarchical systems offer an innovative response to the challenges posed by digital platforms and their impact on power dynamics. By leveraging technology to facilitate open communication, participatory decision-making, and grassroots mobilization, these systems can counteract the tendencies toward centralization and control that often characterize contemporary politics. In this digital age, the potential for non-hierarchical organization becomes a beacon of hope, illuminating pathways toward a more equitable and just society, where individuals are not merely subjects of governance but active agents of change, committed to realizing a shared vision of democracy that honors both human rights and the planet.

THE POWER OF COLLECTIVE ACTION

Collective action stands as a formidable force in the pursuit of justice, equality, and ethical governance. In a world increasingly defined by authoritarianism, oligarchic tendencies, and the erosion of democratic values, the ability of individuals to unite around shared goals becomes an essential tool for reclaiming power. The history of social movements teaches us that when individuals come together, their collective voice has the potential to challenge and dismantle oppressive structures. This unity not only amplifies individual concerns but also cultivates a sense of solidarity that is vital for confronting systemic injustices. As we navigate the complexities of modern governance, embracing the power of collective action becomes essential for fostering change.

The existentialist perspective emphasizes the importance of personal responsibility in democratic engagement. Each individual, by choosing to participate in collective efforts, acknowledges their role in shaping the political landscape. This recognition is critical, as it propels individuals to act not only for themselves but for the broader community. In moments of crisis, such as those posed by authoritarian regimes, the choice to engage in collective action embodies a profound ethical commitment to enhance the rights and freedoms of all. By standing firm together against the encroachment of tyranny, citizens can redefine the parameters of power and assert their right to a more equitable society.

In the context of eco-philosophy, collective action takes on an urgent dimension as we confront environmental degradation and its intersection with social justice. Movements advocating for sustainable governance illustrate how collective efforts can challenge the prevailing paradigms of exploitation and consumption. By reimagining democracy through environmental ethics, communities can foster governance structures that prioritize the health of both the planet and its inhabitants. This holistic approach recognizes that ecological well-being is intrinsically linked to social equity, and it empowers citizens to forge alliances that transcend traditional political boundaries.

Feminist political theory further enriches our understanding of collective action by highlighting the necessity of inclusive governance. By challenging traditional power structures, feminist movements advocate for a political landscape where diverse voices are heard and valued. Such inclusivity not only enriches democratic discourse but also strengthens collective action by ensuring that the needs and experiences of marginalized groups are central to the struggle for justice. In this way, the power of collective action becomes a transformative force, capable of dismantling hierarchies and fostering a more just society.

The rise of digital platforms has redefined the landscape of political engagement, offering new avenues for collective action. These technologies enable individuals to connect, organize, and mobilize in ways previously unimaginable, transcending geographical and social barriers. However, this potential is accompanied by challenges, as the very platforms that empower can also be tools of manipulation and control. It is through critical engagement with technology that we can harness its capabilities for the collective good while remaining vigilant against its abuses. By fostering an environment where ethical considerations guide technological use, we can create a more participatory democracy that honors the collective will of the people.

CRITICAL THEORY AND SOCIAL CHANGE

Culture and Ideology in Political Systems

Culture and ideology serve as the bedrock of political systems, shaping the principles that guide governance and the values that societies hold dear. In the landscape of contemporary politics, where authoritarianism and oligarchic structures threaten the very fabric of democracy, it becomes crucial to reimagine the narratives that define our political engagements. A profound understanding of the cultural contexts and ideological underpinnings allows individuals to confront these oppressive systems with renewed vigor, fostering a collective responsibility to challenge the status quo. By embracing diverse philosophical perspectives, we can cultivate a more inclusive and just political landscape that respects the dignity of every individual.

Existentialism invites us to reflect on personal responsibility within democratic participation. It compels us to consider how our choices shape not only our lives but also the societies we inhabit. As we grapple with the weight of our existence, the call to action becomes clear: we must engage actively in the political process, confront injustices, and advocate for a system that values human rights. This engagement is not merely a civic duty; it is a moral imperative that requires us to stand firm against the encroachment of authoritarianism. By acknowledging our role in shaping political realities, we empower ourselves to envision a future defined by ethical leadership and active citizenship.

Eco-philosophy adds another layer to our understanding of democracy, urging us to rethink governance through the lens of environmental ethics. The climate crisis serves as a stark reminder of the interconnectedness of social justice and ecological sustainability. A political system that neglects its responsibility toward the planet ultimately undermines the rights of its citizens. By integrating eco-centric values into political discourse, we can cultivate a democracy that prioritizes the well-being of both people and the environment. This holistic approach recognizes that true progress cannot occur in isolation; it must embrace the intricate web of relationships that bind us to one another and to the earth.

Feminist political theory challenges traditional power structures, advocating for governance that reflects the diverse experiences and needs of all individuals. By centering marginalized voices, we can dismantle the patriarchal frameworks that often dominate political systems. This inclusivity not only enriches our understanding of democracy but also fosters a culture of empathy and cooperation. As we strive for a more equitable society, we must champion policies and practices that empower women and other underrepresented groups, ensuring that their contributions shape the future of governance. In this way, we can create a political landscape that is truly representative and just.

Finally, the rise of technology and digital platforms has transformed political engagement, presenting both opportunities and challenges. While these tools can facilitate grassroots movements and amplify marginalized voices, they also risk perpetuating existing power dynamics. To navigate this complex terrain, we must critically examine how technology influences political discourse and public participation. By embracing a critical theory approach, we can uncover the cultural ideologies that shape our political systems and work towards social change that transcends traditional hierarchies. In reimagining democracy, we must harness the power of technology to foster authentic engagement, ensuring that every voice is heard and valued in the ongoing quest for justice and equality.

THE ROLE OF ART AND MEDIA IN RESISTANCE

Art and media have historically served as powerful tools in the resistance against authoritarian regimes, transcending the limitations imposed by oppressive political systems. In times of repression, creativity flourishes as a means of expression, allowing individuals and communities to articulate their dissent and envision alternative futures. Through literature, visual arts, music, and digital platforms, artists and activists have the ability to challenge dominant narratives, foster solidarity, and inspire collective action. These mediums not only document the struggles faced by marginalized populations but also ignite the imagination required to reimagine democracy and advocate for social change.

The role of art in political resistance cannot be overstated; it humanizes the abstract concepts of oppression and injustice, making them palpable and relatable. For instance, protest art, whether in the form of murals, poetry, or performance, encapsulates the lived experiences of those resisting authoritarianism. These creative expressions resonate deeply with audiences, encouraging empathy and understanding that transcends geographical and cultural boundaries. Furthermore, art has the unique ability to bypass censorship, creating spaces where dissent can flourish and narratives can be reclaimed. In doing so, it empowers individuals to confront their fears and assert their rights, reinforcing the belief that change is possible.

Media, especially in the digital age, plays a crucial role in amplifying voices that challenge the status quo. Social media platforms have become arenas for political engagement, where individuals can share their experiences, mobilize support, and disseminate information rapidly. This democratization of information allows for a more inclusive discourse, breaking down traditional power structures that often silence dissent. However, the same platforms can also be weaponized by authoritarian regimes to suppress opposition and manipulate public perception. Thus, understanding the duality of technology is essential for harnessing its potential for social change while remaining vigilant against its misuse.

Philosophical engagement with these forms of expression reveals the deeper ethical implications of resistance. Existentialism emphasizes personal responsibility in the face of societal challenges, urging individuals to take a stand against injustices and actively participate in the democratic process. This call to action is echoed in feminist political theory, which advocates for inclusive governance by challenging traditional hierarchies and power structures. By intertwining these philosophical perspectives with artistic and media practices, a robust framework emerges that not only critiques existing systems but also envisions equitable alternatives rooted in justice and sustainability.

In conclusion, the intersection of art, media, and resistance highlights the transformative potential inherent in creative expression. As we confront the realities of authoritarianism and the erosion of human rights, the voices of artists and activists remind us of our shared humanity and the importance of standing firm against oppression. By embracing unconventional philosophies and advocating for a more inclusive and participatory democracy, we can cultivate a landscape where diverse narratives thrive and the collective imagination redefines the boundaries of possibility. This ongoing dialogue between art, media, and resistance will be vital in shaping a future that prioritizes ethical leadership and the flourishing of all individuals within society.

TRANSFORMING CONSCIOUSNESS FOR SOCIAL JUSTICE

Transforming consciousness for social justice requires a profound shift in how we perceive power, authority, and our roles within societal structures. In a world increasingly dominated by authoritarianism and oligarchic systems, it is imperative to cultivate a collective consciousness that prioritizes ethical engagement and inclusivity. This transformation begins with recognizing the interconnectedness of individual actions and broader social movements. By embracing unconventional philosophies, we can reimagine democracy as a living framework that evolves with the needs of its people, ensuring that all voices are heard and valued in the quest for social justice.

As we delve into existentialism, we uncover the individual's responsibility in shaping democratic participation. Each person holds the power to challenge the status quo, to question existing power dynamics, and to advocate for the rights of others. This sense of personal agency is crucial in the fight against dictatorship and the erosion of fundamental human rights. By fostering a culture of critical thinking and active engagement, we empower ourselves and our communities to confront injustice head-on. The act of standing firm against oppressive systems is not merely a political stance; it is a moral imperative that demands courage and a commitment to collective well-being.

Eco-philosophy further enriches our understanding of democracy by intertwining environmental ethics with governance. In recognizing that environmental justice is inherently linked to social justice, we can advocate for sustainable practices that honor the earth and its inhabitants. This perspective challenges traditional power structures that prioritize profit over people and the planet. By rethinking our governance models to incorporate ecological considerations, we pave the way for a more equitable society where the rights of nature and humanity coexist harmoniously, fostering resilience against the ravages of climate change and ecological degradation.

Feminist political theory invites us to challenge the patriarchal underpinnings of our political systems, envisioning an inclusive governance that uplifts marginalized voices. By interrogating historical injustices and advocating for gender equality, we can dismantle the barriers that perpetuate inequality. This approach not only enriches our understanding of democracy but also empowers individuals to engage in transformative actions that promote social equity. In creating spaces where diverse perspectives are valued, we cultivate a more vibrant and just society that reflects the rich tapestry of human experience.

In this era of rapid technological advancement, the intersection of technology and democracy presents both challenges and opportunities. Digital platforms have the potential to democratize information and amplify marginalized voices, yet they can also entrench existing power dynamics and facilitate oppression. By critically analyzing the role of technology in political engagement, we can harness its capabilities for social change while remaining vigilant against its misuse. This critical theory approach encourages us to examine the cultural and ideological forces at play, enabling us to envision a future where technology serves as a tool for justice rather than a mechanism of control. Through this transformative lens, we can reimagine democracy as a dynamic and inclusive system that responds to the needs of all citizens, fostering a renewed commitment to social justice in every aspect of our lives.

UTOPIAN AND DYSTOPIAN VISIONS
Imagining Future Societies

Imagining future societies requires a bold reexamination of our current political frameworks and a commitment to embracing unconventional philosophies that challenge the status quo. As we navigate the complexities of authoritarianism and oligarchical systems, it becomes imperative to envision governance that prioritizes human rights, sustainability, and inclusive participation. By drawing from diverse philosophical traditions, we can create a tapestry of ideas that empowers individuals and communities to reshape their destinies. This vision of democracy transcends mere electoral processes, encouraging active engagement and moral responsibility in the face of systemic oppression.

In this reimagined landscape, eco-philosophy plays a pivotal role in redefining democratic principles through environmental ethics. Future societies must prioritize the health of our planet as an essential component of governance, recognizing that ecological sustainability is intertwined with social justice. By integrating environmental considerations into political decision-making, we can cultivate a society that respects both human and non-human life. This approach not only addresses the urgent climate crisis but also fosters a sense of shared responsibility, urging citizens to act as stewards of their environments while demanding accountability from their leaders.

Furthermore, feminist political theory offers a transformative lens through which to challenge traditional power structures. Envisioning governance that is genuinely inclusive requires dismantling patriarchal norms and practices that have long dominated political discourse. Future societies must embrace diversity in leadership and policy-making, ensuring that marginalized voices are not only heard but actively shape the democratic process. By prioritizing equity and representation, we can create systems that reflect the richness of human experiences and foster a culture of collaboration rather than division.

The influence of technology on democracy cannot be understated, as digital platforms continue to reshape political engagement and power dynamics. Imagining future societies involves critically assessing the role of technology in amplifying voices and facilitating grassroots movements. While these tools offer unprecedented opportunities for connection and mobilization, they also pose challenges that must be addressed to prevent the erosion of democratic ideals. By cultivating a digital landscape that values transparency and ethical practices, we can harness technology as a force for social change, empowering individuals to reclaim their agency in the political sphere.

Ultimately, the existential responsibility of individuals in democratic participation cannot be overlooked. As we confront the realities of limited rights and the abuse of power, it is essential to foster a culture of active citizenship. This requires not only awareness and education but also the courage to challenge oppressive systems. By embracing a diverse array of philosophical perspectives, we can imagine future societies that not only resist authoritarianism but also actively promote justice, equity, and sustainability. In this endeavor, each person holds the potential to contribute to a more just and compassionate world, realizing that the path to meaningful change begins with our collective imagination and unwavering commitment to moral leadership.

THE ROLE OF ETHICS IN POLITICAL LEADERSHIP

Defining Moral Responsibilities

Moral responsibilities in the context of political leadership are foundational to the pursuit of justice and the protection of human dignity. In an era where authoritarianism threatens the democratic fabric of society, leaders must embrace a philosophy that transcends mere governance. Moral leadership requires an unwavering commitment to ethical principles, ensuring that decisions reflect the highest standards of integrity and respect for human rights. This commitment demands that leaders not only articulate a vision of a better society but also embody the values that underpin that vision, engaging actively in the promotion of democratic ideals.

Understanding moral responsibilities involves recognizing the interplay between individual actions and collective outcomes. Each leader must grapple with the existential weight of their decisions, acknowledging that their choices can either fortify or dismantle the structures of power that govern society. This awareness calls for a proactive stance against the encroachment of authoritarianism, where silence and inaction can lead to complicity. Moral leaders must inspire others to engage in democratic participation, cultivating an environment where every voice contributes to the collective narrative, thus redefining what it means to be a responsible citizen in an ever-evolving political landscape.

The integration of eco-philosophy into the discourse of moral responsibilities further enriches our understanding of governance. As we confront the existential crises of climate change and environmental degradation, leaders are tasked with the moral obligation to advocate for sustainable practices that honor both the planet and its inhabitants. This responsibility extends beyond immediate political concerns; it encompasses a holistic view of our interconnectedness with nature and the ethical imperatives that arise from this relationship. By prioritizing ecological stewardship, leaders can forge a path toward a more inclusive and sustainable democracy that respects the rights of future generations.

Moreover, feminist political theory challenges traditional power structures by emphasizing the need for inclusive governance that reflects diverse perspectives. Moral responsibilities in this realm require leaders to dismantle systems of oppression and advocate for equality, ensuring that marginalized voices are not only heard but actively integrated into the decision-making process. This approach reimagines democracy as a living, breathing entity that evolves through the contributions of all its constituents, fostering a culture of mutual respect and collaboration in the face of systemic challenges.

Lastly, as technology reshapes the landscape of political engagement, leaders must navigate the ethical implications of digital platforms in their governance. The responsibility to harness technology for the greater good is paramount, as it can either empower citizens or perpetuate existing inequalities. Moral leadership in this context involves critically analyzing the impact of technology on political dynamics, advocating for transparency, and fostering digital literacy among the populace. By embracing an ethical framework that prioritizes human rights and democratic values, leaders can steer society toward a future where power is decentralized, and collective agency thrives, ultimately redefining what it means to lead with integrity in an age of uncertainty.

CULTIVATING INTEGRITY IN LEADERSHIP

Cultivating integrity in leadership is not merely a noble aspiration; it is an essential foundation for any society striving to reclaim its democratic values. In an age where authoritarianism and oligarchic systems threaten to undermine the very fabric of our collective existence, leaders must embody integrity as a beacon of hope. This commitment to ethical principles fosters trust and accountability, creating a political environment where citizens feel empowered to engage meaningfully in democratic processes. By prioritizing integrity, leaders can inspire a resurgence of civic responsibility and rekindle the belief that individual actions matter in the collective fight against oppression.

Integrity in leadership also requires an unwavering commitment to transparency. In a world rife with misinformation and manipulation, leaders must not only communicate their intentions clearly but also demonstrate their dedication to ethical decision-making. This transparency dismantles the barriers that often separate leaders from the people they serve, hence promoting an inclusive dialogue that honors diverse perspectives. It is through this open exchange that integrity flourishes, allowing communities to engage in a shared vision for a more just society. When leaders exemplify transparency, they cultivate a culture of accountability that encourages citizens to hold their government accountable as well.

Furthermore, the cultivation of integrity in leadership invites an exploration of personal responsibility within the broader context of democratic engagement. Each individual has a role to play in shaping the political landscape, and leaders must inspire this sense of responsibility by modeling ethical behavior. The existentialist perspective emphasizes the importance of individual action, urging citizens to confront the consequences of their choices. When leaders embody integrity, they not only challenge the status quo but also empower others to take ownership of their political agency. This interconnectedness between leadership and personal responsibility is crucial in dismantling the structures of power that perpetuate injustice.

In addition to personal responsibility, the integration of eco-philosophy and sustainable governance into leadership practices underscores the necessity of ethical considerations in our political systems. As we grapple with pressing environmental crises, leaders must cultivate integrity by prioritizing ecological stewardship and sustainable practices. By aligning their policies with the principles of environmental ethics, leaders can reimagine democracy as a system that respects both humanity and the planet. This holistic approach to governance champions the interconnectedness of social issues and ecological well-being, fostering a moral imperative for inclusive and sustainable political action.

Ultimately, cultivating integrity in leadership is a transformative endeavor that challenges traditional power structures while envisioning a more equitable future. By drawing from diverse philosophical frameworks, leaders can foster a political climate that honors human rights, embraces inclusivity, and champions ethical governance. As communities rally together to stand firm against authoritarianism, the cultivation of integrity becomes an act of resistance and resilience. In this pursuit, leaders not only uphold their moral responsibilities but also inspire a collective awakening—a movement toward a democracy that truly reflects the will and dignity of its people.

PATHS TO MORAL LEADERSHIP
Personal Transformation and Political Engagement

Personal transformation is an essential precursor to meaningful political engagement, particularly in a world increasingly characterized by authoritarianism and oligarchic structures. As individuals undergo profound changes in their understanding of ethics, responsibility, and their role in society, they become empowered to challenge the status quo. This process of self-discovery and realization fosters a commitment to democratic ideals that transcend traditional notions of governance. It invites individuals to embrace their capacity for agency, urging them to participate actively in shaping the political landscape instead of remaining passive observers in a system that often feels alien and oppressive.

In the context of existentialism, the notion of personal responsibility becomes paramount. Each person's engagement in democratic processes is not merely a right but a moral duty that reflects their values and beliefs. This philosophical perspective challenges individuals to confront their own complicity in existing power structures. By recognizing that their choices contribute to the collective outcome, individuals can catalyze change not only within themselves but also in their communities. The act of voting, protesting, or advocating for policy changes transforms from a mundane task into a profound expression of one's ethical convictions, highlighting the intrinsic link between personal transformation and political activism.

Furthermore, eco-philosophy introduces a vital dimension to this discourse, urging us to rethink democracy through the lens of environmental ethics. As awareness of climate change and ecological degradation intensifies, individuals are called to reflect on their relationship with the planet and the implications of governmental policies on environmental sustainability. This reflection often leads to a transformative realization that social change cannot be divorced from ecological responsibility. A commitment to sustainable governance becomes a natural extension of personal transformation, inspiring individuals to engage politically in ways that prioritize both human and environmental rights.

The feminist political theory framework provides another critical lens through which to explore personal transformation in political engagement. It challenges traditional power structures that have historically marginalized voices based on gender, race, and class. As individuals embrace feminist principles, they are inspired to advocate for inclusive governance that reflects the diverse tapestry of society. This transformative journey encourages a rejection of hierarchical systems and promotes solidarity among marginalized communities, fostering a political landscape where everyone has a stake and a voice in shaping their collective future.

Finally, the intersection of technology and democracy presents new avenues for personal transformation and political engagement. Digital platforms have revolutionized the way individuals connect, organize, and advocate for change. The democratization of information empowers citizens to challenge authoritarian narratives and mobilize grassroots movements. However, it also requires a critical examination of the implications of these technologies on power dynamics and individual agency. As individuals navigate this digital landscape, they must remain vigilant about the ethical responsibilities that come with newfound capabilities, ensuring that their engagement is not only impactful but also aligned with the principles of justice, equity, and sustainability. Through this multifaceted lens, personal transformation emerges as a powerful catalyst for political engagement, fostering a more profound commitment to reimagining democracy in our contemporary world.

THE FUTURE OF ETHICAL LEADERSHIP IN GOVERNANCE

The future of ethical leadership in governance demands a profound reimagining of our democratic principles, transcending conventional structures that have long dictated the political landscape. In an era marked by the rise of authoritarianism and oligarchic tendencies, leaders must embody a commitment to transparency, accountability, and inclusivity. Ethical leadership, rooted in moral philosophy, becomes pivotal as it compels individuals in power to prioritize the collective well-being over personal or party interests. This transformative approach not only fosters trust among citizens but also encourages active participation in the democratic process, essential for safeguarding fundamental rights against encroaching authoritarianism.

As we navigate the complexities of contemporary governance, the integration of eco-philosophy and sustainable practices into leadership paradigms emerges as a vital aspect of ethical stewardship. Leaders who embrace environmental ethics are better equipped to address the pressing challenges of climate change and ecological degradation, ensuring that policies reflect the interdependence of social and environmental health. By championing sustainable governance, ethical leaders can inspire a cultural shift that values long-term ecological integrity over short-term gains, establishing a new norm where environmental considerations are integral to political decision-making. This holistic approach not only enhances the quality of life for present generations but also secures a livable future for those yet to come.

Furthermore, the exploration of feminist political theory offers a crucial lens through which to challenge traditional power structures. Ethical leadership must include diverse perspectives, particularly those of marginalized groups, to cultivate a more inclusive governance model. By addressing systemic inequalities and promoting equitable representation, leaders can dismantle the patriarchal underpinnings of political systems and create space for innovative solutions that reflect the needs of all constituents. This paradigm shift not only empowers individuals but also enriches the democratic process, fostering a society where every voice is valued and every citizen has the opportunity to contribute to the collective narrative.

In addition to these philosophical frameworks, the impact of technology on political engagement cannot be overlooked. Ethical leaders must navigate the digital landscape with discernment, recognizing both the opportunities and challenges presented by social media and online platforms. By promoting digital literacy and responsible engagement, leaders can harness technology as a tool for empowerment rather than manipulation. This involves fostering environments where citizens can engage in meaningful dialogue, share diverse viewpoints, and mobilize for social change, ultimately reinforcing the foundations of a vibrant democracy in the face of rising authoritarian pressures.

Ultimately, the future of ethical leadership in governance hinges on a collective commitment to uphold human rights and cultivate a culture of responsibility among citizens. As we confront the dangers of limited rights and the abuse of power, it is imperative that individuals take an active role in shaping their political realities. By engaging with critical theory and envisioning both utopian and dystopian futures, we can challenge the status quo and inspire a new generation of leaders dedicated to ethical governance. In doing so, we not only reclaim our democratic ideals but also pave the way for a society that truly reflects our shared values and aspirations for justice, equity, and sustainability.

PHILOSOPHY OF RIGHTS IN CONTEMPORARY POLITICS

Human Rights as a Foundation for Governance

Human rights serve as the bedrock of governance, influencing the structures and principles that define political authority and societal well-being. In a world fraught with authoritarianism and oligarchic tendencies, the recognition and protection of human rights are not merely legal obligations; they are moral imperatives that frame our understanding of justice, equality, and freedom. This foundational perspective invites us to interrogate the very nature of governance, prompting a shift from rigid hierarchies to more inclusive frameworks that honor the inherent dignity of every individual. By embracing human rights, we can challenge the status quo and envision a governance model that prioritizes the well-being of all citizens, particularly those marginalized by existing power structures.

The philosophical underpinnings of human rights compel us to engage with notions of personal responsibility and collective action. In democratic participation, each individual bears the weight of their choices and must recognize their role in shaping the political landscape. This existential engagement is vital; it reminds us that apathy in the face of injustice contributes to the perpetuation of authoritarian regimes. A conscious citizenry, aware of their rights and responsibilities, can resist oppression and advocate for a governance model that reflects the values of equity and justice. This active participation not only empowers individuals but also fosters a culture where human rights are respected and upheld, reinforcing the ethical dimensions of leadership.

In the context of contemporary governance, eco-philosophy offers a transformative lens through which to view human rights. As we grapple with environmental crises, the interconnectedness of rights becomes evident. The right to a healthy environment is intrinsically linked to other human rights, emphasizing a holistic approach to governance that integrates environmental ethics into political decision-making. By reimagining democracy through these principles, we can cultivate a sustainable future that respects both human dignity and ecological balance, ensuring that governance serves the interests of the planet as well as its inhabitants.

Feminist political theory further enriches the discourse on human rights and governance by challenging traditional power structures that perpetuate inequality. The movement for inclusive governance calls for the dismantling of patriarchal systems that marginalize voices and experiences of women and other disenfranchised groups. By incorporating feminist perspectives into the governance framework, we can foster a more equitable society that recognizes the diverse experiences of all individuals. This reimagining is not merely an academic exercise; it is a call to arms for those who seek to challenge the oppressive dynamics of power and advocate for a democratic system that values inclusivity and justice.

Lastly, as we navigate the complexities of technology and its impact on democracy, the role of human rights becomes increasingly critical. Digital platforms hold the potential to enhance political engagement, yet they also pose risks to privacy and freedom of expression. The governance of technology must be grounded in a commitment to human rights, ensuring that these tools serve to empower rather than suppress. By integrating a rights-based approach into our technological frameworks, we can safeguard democratic participation and cultivate an environment where citizens engage meaningfully in the political process.

The commitment to human rights as a foundation for governance not only strengthens our democratic ideals but also inspires a collective movement toward a just and equitable future.

THE IMPLICATIONS OF LIMITED RIGHTS

The implications of limited rights extend far beyond the individual, permeating the very fabric of society and shaping the political landscape in profound ways. When rights are constricted, the potential for human creativity, expression, and participation diminishes, leading to a culture of fear and compliance. This erosion of rights creates an environment where authoritarianism thrives, stifling dissent and nurturing a populace that feels disempowered and disengaged. The interplay between limited rights and moral leadership becomes critical, as the failure to advocate for expansive freedoms not only undermines personal agency but also invites a future where oppression becomes normalized.

In the realm of existentialism, the struggle against limited rights reflects a deeper inquiry into personal responsibility and ethical engagement. Each individual is called to confront their own role within these oppressive structures, examining how their choices either contribute to or challenge the status quo. Embracing existentialist thought encourages active participation in democratic processes, urging individuals to reclaim their agency and resist complacency. The act of standing firm against authoritarian regimes requires a recognition that one's voice matters, and that collective action can catalyze significant change. This philosophical engagement is essential in reimagining a democracy that is vibrant, inclusive, and responsive to the needs of all citizens.

Eco-philosophy brings another vital perspective to the conversation, highlighting the interconnectedness of environmental ethics and governance. As limited rights often lead to the exploitation of both people and the planet, a rethinking of democratic frameworks is necessary to prioritize sustainability and equitable resource distribution. A governance model that respects the rights of individuals while recognizing the moral imperative to protect the environment can foster a society that values both human dignity and ecological balance. This holistic approach to democracy can empower marginalized communities, ensuring that their voices are integral to the decision-making processes that shape their futures.

Feminist political theory challenges the traditional power structures that frequently accompany limited rights, advocating for a more inclusive and equitable governance model. By interrogating the intersections of gender, race, and class, feminist thinkers illuminate the ways in which authoritarian systems disproportionately affect vulnerable populations. The call for a more democratic society is not just about the expansion of rights, but also about creating a political landscape that genuinely reflects the diversity of experiences and perspectives. This vision demands that we dismantle oppressive hierarchies and build systems that empower all individuals, enabling them to engage fully in the political process.

Finally, the impact of technology on democracy cannot be understated, as digital platforms have transformed the dynamics of political engagement. While these tools can facilitate communication and mobilization, they also pose risks of manipulation and control by those in power. The challenge lies in harnessing technology to enhance democratic participation while remaining vigilant against its potential abuses. As we navigate this complex terrain, it is essential to advocate for transparency, accountability, and ethical standards that uphold the rights of individuals. In reimagining democracy, we must embrace innovative approaches that empower citizens and foster a culture of active, informed engagement, ensuring that the implications of limited rights are addressed with urgency and resolve.

STRATEGIES FOR ADVOCACY AND CHANGE

In the struggle against authoritarianism and the pervasive influence of oligarchic systems, advocacy and change must be rooted in a profound understanding of the complexities of power dynamics. To foster meaningful transformation, individuals must engage in a multifaceted approach that integrates various philosophical frameworks. Embracing existentialism encourages personal responsibility in political participation, urging citizens to confront their own roles within democratic systems. Each act of civic engagement, no matter how small, contributes to a collective movement that can dismantle oppressive structures and promote a more inclusive and just society.

The integration of eco-philosophy into advocacy strategies offers a compelling perspective on sustainable governance. By aligning environmental ethics with democratic principles, activists can articulate a vision of democracy that prioritizes ecological stewardship and the well-being of future generations. This approach not only challenges existing power hierarchies but also emphasizes the interconnectedness of social justice and environmental health. Advocates can mobilize communities around the shared goal of preserving the planet, thereby fostering solidarity and empowering marginalized voices often silenced in traditional political discourse.

Feminist political theory provides critical insights into the ways traditional power structures can be deconstructed to create more inclusive governance. By centering the experiences and perspectives of marginalized gender identities, advocates can challenge the patriarchal underpinnings of current systems. This reimagining of democracy calls for the incorporation of diverse voices into decision-making processes, ensuring that policies reflect the needs and aspirations of all citizens. Such a shift not only enriches democratic processes but also strengthens the fabric of society by promoting equality and justice.

Post-colonial perspectives further enhance our understanding of democracy by revealing the historical injustices that continue to shape contemporary governance. Advocacy must therefore involve a critical examination of the legacies of colonialism and the ongoing effects of systemic oppression. By addressing these historical grievances, activists can work toward a reclamation of agency for those who have been marginalized. This approach fosters a political landscape where diverse narratives are acknowledged and respected, paving the way for a more equitable society that honors all histories.

In the digital age, the intersection of technology and democracy presents both challenges and opportunities for advocacy. Digital platforms can serve as powerful tools for mobilization and engagement, allowing individuals to connect, share ideas, and organize collective action. However, it is essential to remain vigilant against the potential for these platforms to perpetuate authoritarianism and restrict freedom of expression. Advocates must harness the power of technology to create transparent, accountable systems that empower citizens and promote active participation in governance. By fostering a culture of critical engagement with technology, individuals can reclaim their rights and reshape the political landscape toward a more democratic future.

BUILDING COMMUNITIES OF RESISTANCE

Building communities of resistance is essential in the face of rising authoritarianism and the erosion of democratic values. These communities emerge from a shared understanding of the ethical imperative to challenge oppressive systems. They are spaces where individuals come together to articulate their dissent, drawing inspiration from diverse philosophical traditions that prioritize human dignity and collective action. Through dialogue and collaboration, these communities can forge new pathways toward a more just society, grounded in the principles of equality, respect, and compassion.

In exploring the philosophical underpinnings of resistance, we find that existentialism offers a powerful lens for understanding personal responsibility in political engagement. Each individual is called to confront their own role within a system that may perpetuate injustice. This realization lays the groundwork for a communal ethic of resistance, where personal agency is celebrated and encouraged. By embracing the belief that our choices matter, we empower ourselves and others to stand firm against the forces that seek to diminish our rights and freedoms.

Furthermore, eco-philosophy invites us to rethink democracy in light of environmental ethics. The interconnectedness of social justice and ecological sustainability is becoming increasingly clear as we recognize that the health of our planet is inextricably linked to the well-being of our communities. Building communities of resistance in this context means advocating for governance that honors both human rights and environmental stewardship. Together, we can cultivate a vision of democracy that prioritizes the earth and its inhabitants, ensuring that future generations inherit a world worth fighting for.

Feminist political theory also plays a crucial role in challenging traditional power structures. By centering the experiences and voices of marginalized groups, we can create inclusive governance that values diversity and equity. Communities of resistance informed by feminist thought are not merely reactive; they actively seek to reshape political discourse and practice, making space for those who have historically been silenced. This holistic approach to resistance embraces the complexities of identity and power, fostering solidarity among different movements striving for justice.

Lastly, the emergence of technology in political engagement presents both challenges and opportunities. Digital platforms can amplify voices and mobilize communities, serving as vital tools for resistance. However, we must remain vigilant about the ways technology can also reinforce existing power dynamics. Building communities of resistance requires a critical examination of how we engage with technology, ensuring it serves democratic ideals rather than undermines them. In this evolving landscape, we must harness the potential of digital spaces while committing to ethical principles that guide our collective action against authoritarianism and uphold the rights of all individuals.

THE ROLE OF HOPE IN POLITICAL ACTIVISM

Hope serves as a powerful catalyst in political activism, invigorating individuals and communities to challenge oppressive systems and strive for a more just society. In an environment often dominated by despair and cynicism, hope emerges as a beacon that encourages people to envision a world where democracy is not just an ideal but a lived reality. It inspires activists to confront authoritarianism and oligarchic structures, reminding them that change is possible even in the face of overwhelming odds. This sense of hope fuels the belief that collective action can dismantle the barriers imposed by those in power and reimagine governance in a way that prioritizes human rights, equity, and sustainability.

The intertwining of hope and personal responsibility is particularly salient in existentialist thought, which emphasizes the role of individuals in shaping their destinies. Activists, when driven by hope, recognize their agency in political engagement, understanding that their actions can influence the trajectory of their communities. This sense of responsibility transcends mere participation in democratic processes; it embodies a commitment to confront injustices, challenge the status quo, and advocate for those whose voices have been marginalized. By embracing hope, individuals can transform their existential angst into purposeful action, fostering a culture of resilience and determination that empowers collective movements for change.

Furthermore, hope is essential in fostering a vision for sustainable governance that aligns with eco-philosophy. As activists grapple with the pressing challenges of climate change and environmental degradation, hope enables them to reimagine political systems that prioritize ecological integrity and social justice. This vision challenges traditional power structures, advocating for inclusive governance that recognizes the interconnectedness of human rights and environmental rights. In this regard, hope becomes a driving force behind innovative solutions and grassroots movements that seek to create a future where both people and the planet can thrive.

In exploring diverse political theories, hope emerges as a unifying theme that transcends disciplines and perspectives. Feminist political theory, for example, harnesses hope to challenge patriarchal norms and promote inclusive governance that values diverse voices and experiences. Similarly, post-colonial perspectives on democracy highlight the necessity of hope in addressing historical injustices and envisioning systems that honor the dignity and rights of all individuals. Within this broader context, hope acts as a common thread that binds various movements, encouraging collaboration and solidarity among those who envision a more equitable and just society.

Ultimately, the role of hope in political activism underscores the importance of ethical leadership and moral responsibility. As individuals and movements confront the complexities of modern governance, including the influence of technology and the challenges posed by authoritarianism, hope remains a vital ingredient for fostering engagement and inspiring action. It empowers individuals to dream of a better tomorrow, reminding them that their efforts can lead to transformative social change. In this way, hope is not merely an abstract ideal but a practical necessity for those navigating the tumultuous landscape of contemporary politics, guiding them toward a future defined by justice, equity, and shared humanity.

POWER DYNAMICS: UNDERSTANDING POLITICAL SYSTEMS AND THEIR IMPACT ON SOCIETY

THE FOUNDATIONS OF POLITICAL SYSTEMS

Political systems serve as the bedrock upon which societies are built, shaping the lives of individuals and communities in profound ways. Understanding these systems is crucial, as they influence everything from governance to economic opportunities and social justice. At the core of political systems lies the interplay between power and the structures that maintain it. This interplay determines not only who wields authority but also how that authority is exercised, often dictating the quality of life for citizens and the health of the society they inhabit. For adults navigating today's complex world, grasping the foundations of political systems is essential for fostering informed civic engagement and promoting accountability.

The concept of oligarchy, where a small group holds power over the many, exemplifies how political systems can lead to significant disparities in wealth and influence. In oligarchic societies, economic inequality tends to flourish, as those in power prioritize their interests over the common good. The concentration of wealth and resources in the hands of a few can stifle innovation, limit opportunities for the masses, and create a cycle of disenfranchisement. Addressing the impact of oligarchy on economic inequality is not just an academic exercise; it is a call to action for individuals and communities to advocate for more equitable governance structures that empower rather than suppress.

Human rights advocacy is another critical component of understanding political systems, especially within authoritarian regimes where freedoms are often curtailed. The struggle for human rights is a universal endeavor, transcending borders and cultures. Supporting individuals and organizations that champion these rights is vital in fostering resilience against oppression. By engaging with and promoting human rights advocacy, adults contribute to a culture of accountability, demanding that governments respect and uphold the inherent dignity of every person. This commitment not only helps those suffering under authoritarian rule but also reinforces the foundations of a healthy society that values justice and equality.

Political education and civic engagement are essential for empowering youth to navigate and influence political landscapes. A well-informed populace is the cornerstone of any functioning democracy, enabling citizens to challenge injustices and advocate for meaningful change. By investing in political education, communities can inspire the next generation to actively participate in civic life, equipping them with the tools to question, engage, and ultimately reshape their political environments. This engagement is not only beneficial for the youth themselves but for society as a whole, as fresh ideas and perspectives can lead to innovative solutions for longstanding issues.

Finally, the role of international organizations in promoting human rights cannot be overlooked. These entities serve as vital advocates for justice, supporting initiatives that encourage political reform and protect the most vulnerable populations. Through comparative analyses of different political systems, including democracies and oligarchies, we can gain insights into best practices and strategies for fostering human rights globally. Historical case studies of tyranny and resistance illustrate the enduring human spirit in the face of oppression, reminding us that change is possible. By understanding the foundations of political systems and their impacts, we empower ourselves and our communities to strive for a more just and equitable world, even in the face of adversity.

THE ROLE OF GOVERNANCE IN SOCIETY

Governance serves as the backbone of society, shaping the frameworks within which individuals and communities operate. Effective governance is fundamental in establishing the rule of law, protecting human rights, and ensuring that all voices are heard in the political arena. When governance is transparent and accountable, it fosters trust between the government and the governed, creating an environment where citizens feel empowered to participate in decision-making processes. This engagement is crucial, particularly in times of adversity, as it encourages resilience and solidarity among the populace, enabling societies to navigate challenges collectively.

In examining the impact of governance on social justice, it becomes evident that political systems directly influence the equitable distribution of resources and opportunities. Democratic systems, with their emphasis on participation and representation, tend to promote social justice more effectively than oligarchies or authoritarian regimes. However, even within democracies, power imbalances can emerge, leading to the concentration of wealth and influence among a select few. This highlights the importance of vigilance and active civic engagement, as citizens must hold their leaders accountable to ensure that governance serves the broader interests of society rather than the elite.

Oligarchies pose a significant threat to economic equality, as they often prioritize the interests of a small group over the welfare of the majority. The concentration of power in the hands of a few can lead to policies that exacerbate inequality, stifling opportunities for social mobility and growth for the wider population. Understanding the dynamics of power within these systems is crucial for advocating for change. By raising awareness about the negative impacts of oligarchic governance, individuals and organizations can mobilize efforts to promote more equitable policies and challenge the status quo.

Human rights advocacy plays a vital role in societies governed by authoritarian regimes, where dissent is often met with repression. In these contexts, governance can become a tool for oppression rather than empowerment. Advocates for human rights must work tirelessly to shine a light on abuses and to support those who resist tyranny. The resilience of individuals and organizations in these environments can inspire broader movements for change, demonstrating that the human spirit can thrive even in the darkest of circumstances. International organizations also play a pivotal role in this struggle, providing support and resources to local activists and amplifying their voices on a global stage.

Ultimately, the role of governance in society is intertwined with the aspirations of its citizens. Political education and civic engagement are essential components of a healthy society, empowering individuals to understand their rights and responsibilities within the political framework. By fostering a culture of informed participation, societies can cultivate the leaders of tomorrow who will champion social justice and human rights. As we reflect on historical case studies of tyranny and resistance, we recognize that governance is not merely a system of rules but a living, evolving entity that reflects the collective will and aspirations of its people. It is through active participation and advocacy that societies can strive for a future where governance uplifts rather than suppresses, ensuring that all individuals can thrive.

NAVIGATING POLITICAL LANDSCAPES

Navigating the intricate pathways of political landscapes requires a deep understanding of the systems that govern societies. At the core of this journey lies the need to comprehend political organizations and their influence on the fabric of our communities. By recognizing the dynamics at play within various political systems, individuals can engage more effectively in the dialogue surrounding governance. It is essential to grasp how concepts such as oligarchy and tyranny shape not only policy but also the lived experiences of citizens. As we confront these realities, fostering a commitment to human rights becomes pivotal in creating a society that not only survives but thrives, even in adversity.

The impact of oligarchy on economic inequality is a pressing concern that cannot be overlooked. When power is concentrated in the hands of a few, the gap between the wealthy elite and the average citizen widens, leading to systemic injustices. This concentration of wealth translates into a disproportionate influence over political processes and decision-making, further entrenching inequality. By understanding these patterns, we empower ourselves to challenge the status quo and advocate for policies that promote equitable distribution of resources. A society that values economic justice is one that enables all its members to flourish, underscoring the importance of collective action in the face of entrenched power structures.

In authoritarian regimes, the struggle for human rights often becomes a defining battleground. Advocacy in such environments is fraught with challenges, yet it is crucial for the preservation of dignity and freedom. Those who dare to speak out against tyranny become beacons of hope, inspiring others to join the fight for justice. Supporting these advocates, both locally and globally, is vital for fostering a culture of resilience and empowerment. By amplifying their voices and sharing their stories, we not only raise awareness but also build solidarity in the pursuit of fundamental rights that should be afforded to all.

Political education and civic engagement are essential tools for nurturing a generation that is informed and active. By equipping youth with the knowledge of political systems and the importance of their participation, we lay the groundwork for a more engaged citizenry. Understanding the relationship between political systems and social justice enables young people to critically assess their environments and advocate for change. By fostering environments that encourage discussion and activism, we inspire the leaders of tomorrow to navigate political landscapes with courage and conviction.

The role of international organizations in promoting human rights cannot be underestimated. These entities serve as crucial watchdogs and advocates, pushing for accountability in the face of oppression. Their efforts to highlight the plight of individuals living under tyrannical regimes illuminate the struggles that often go unnoticed. Through comparative analyses of oligarchies and democracies, we gain valuable insights into the mechanisms of power and resistance. Historical case studies of tyranny and the resulting movements for freedom remind us that while the road may be fraught with challenges, the pursuit of justice is a timeless endeavor that must be embraced with unwavering resolve. Together, by navigating these political landscapes, we can build a brighter, more just future for all.

POLITICAL ORGANIZATIONS AND THEIR INFLUENCE
Types of Political Organizations

Political organizations play a pivotal role in shaping the political landscape of societies around the world. They can take various forms, including political parties, interest groups, non-governmental organizations (NGOs), and grassroots movements. Each of these organizations serves distinct purposes, but they all share a common goal: to influence policy, mobilize citizens, and advocate for specific ideologies or interests. Understanding these types of organizations is crucial for individuals striving to navigate the complexities of political systems and engage meaningfully in civic life. By recognizing the functions and impacts of different political entities, adults can empower themselves to participate in the democratic process and advocate for human rights, social justice, and economic equity.

Political parties are perhaps the most recognized type of political organization. They typically aim to gain control over the government by winning elections and implementing their platforms. Parties not only represent specific ideologies but also serve as vehicles for political engagement, providing a structured way for citizens to express their political preferences. In democratic systems, parties encourage competition and debate, fostering an environment where diverse voices can be heard. However, when parties become entrenched in oligarchic practices, they can contribute to economic inequality and limit the representation of marginalized groups, highlighting the importance of active civic engagement to counteract such trends.

Interest groups, another vital type of political organization, advocate for specific issues or causes, ranging from environmental protection to labor rights. These organizations often engage in lobbying efforts, aiming to influence policymakers and shape public opinion. Their effectiveness can vary, as some interest groups possess significant resources and connections, while others may struggle to be heard. Nevertheless, they play a crucial role in raising awareness about pressing social issues and mobilizing public support. Understanding the dynamics of interest groups can equip individuals with the knowledge to support initiatives that align with their values and promote a more just society.

Non-governmental organizations (NGOs) represent a diverse spectrum of political organizations dedicated to various causes, including human rights advocacy, environmental sustainability, and social justice. NGOs often operate on a global scale, forming coalitions that transcend national borders to address issues like climate change and humanitarian crises. Their work is vital in holding governments accountable, especially in authoritarian regimes where human rights abuses may occur. Engaging with and supporting NGOs can empower individuals to contribute to meaningful change and advocate for the rights of those who are marginalized or oppressed.

Grassroots movements exemplify the powerful role that ordinary citizens can play in shaping political discourse and demanding change. These organizations often arise in response to social injustices or political grievances, relying on community engagement and collective action to bring about reform. The rise of grassroots movements has been evident in various historical contexts, showcasing the potential for resistance against tyranny and the fight for democracy. Adults who understand the significance of grassroots activism can inspire future generations to engage in political education and civic participation, fostering a society that values justice, accountability, and human rights for all.

THE POWER OF POLITICAL MOBILIZATION

The power of political mobilization lies in its ability to transform individual voices into a resounding chorus that can demand change, challenge injustices, and reshape the very fabric of society. In an era where the forces of oligarchy and tyranny often seek to silence dissent, the collective action of citizens becomes an essential tool for asserting human rights and advocating for a more equitable society. Political mobilization empowers individuals to recognize their agency, fostering a sense of responsibility and urgency to engage in the political process. It cultivates a culture of civic engagement, where the youth are not mere spectators but active participants, ready to challenge the status quo and fight for social justice.

The historical landscape is replete with examples where organized movements have successfully confronted oppressive regimes, illuminating the path to resistance. From the civil rights movement in the United States to the Arab Spring, political mobilization has proven to be a formidable force against tyranny. These case studies reveal that when individuals unite under a common cause, they can alter the trajectory of their nations, dismantling systems of oppression and advocating for the rights of the marginalized. Such movements not only highlight the resilience of the human spirit but also underscore the necessity of understanding political systems to navigate the complexities of social change.

In the face of economic inequality exacerbated by oligarchic structures, political mobilization serves as a counterbalance, enabling communities to advocate for policies that promote equity and justice. By harnessing the collective strength of citizens, political organizations can influence policymaking, pushing for reforms that address the disparities created by concentrated wealth and power. Grassroots movements often emerge as powerful catalysts for change, drawing attention to issues that may otherwise remain hidden in the shadows of political discourse. Through strategic advocacy and mobilization, citizens can hold their leaders accountable and demand a more just allocation of resources.

The role of international organizations in promoting human rights further illustrates the importance of political mobilization on a global scale. These entities often depend on the grassroots efforts of citizens to bring attention to human rights violations in authoritarian regimes. By collaborating with local activists and organizations, international bodies can amplify their voices, providing them with the necessary resources and platforms to effect change. This synergy between local mobilization and international support creates a robust network that champions human rights, fostering a global community committed to justice and equity.

Ultimately, the power of political mobilization lies in its capacity to inspire hope and action in the face of adversity. It serves as a reminder that even in the darkest times, individuals can come together to challenge oppression, advocate for their rights, and build a healthier society. By understanding the dynamics of political systems and the impact of organized movements, people can equip themselves with the tools necessary to navigate and influence their political landscapes. Empowered citizens are the bedrock of democracy, and through their collective action, they can construct a future where human rights are upheld, and social justice prevails.

STRATEGIES FOR EFFECTIVE ADVOCACY

Advocacy is a powerful tool for individuals and groups seeking to influence political systems and create meaningful change. To navigate the complexities of political organizations and their impact on society, advocates must employ effective strategies that resonate with diverse audiences. One fundamental approach is to build coalitions that unite various stakeholders, including marginalized communities, civil society organizations, and even sympathetic factions within political institutions. By fostering alliances, advocates can amplify their voices, share resources, and create a robust platform for promoting human rights and social justice, especially in times of adversity.

Education plays a pivotal role in advocacy efforts. Empowering individuals with knowledge about political systems, the dynamics of oligarchy and tyranny, and their implications for human rights is essential. Workshops, seminars, and community outreach programs can help demystify complex political concepts, enabling citizens to engage critically with the issues that affect their lives. By equipping people with the tools to understand the relationship between political systems and social justice, advocates can inspire a generation committed to civic engagement and active participation in the democratic process.

Utilizing storytelling is another powerful strategy that can enhance advocacy efforts. Personal narratives humanize abstract political concepts and resonate emotionally with audiences. By sharing real-life stories of individuals impacted by oligarchy or authoritarian regimes, advocates can evoke empathy and mobilize public support for their causes. These stories can serve as compelling testimonies that highlight the urgency of addressing economic inequality and human rights violations, making it clear that advocacy is not merely a political exercise but a moral imperative that calls for collective action.

Advocates should also leverage technology and social media to broaden their reach and enhance engagement. In an increasingly interconnected world, digital platforms offer powerful opportunities to connect with audiences, share information, and mobilize support quickly. Social media campaigns can raise awareness about issues, facilitate discussions, and encourage grassroots organizing. Moreover, online petitions and crowdfunding initiatives can empower individuals to take tangible action, ensuring that advocacy efforts remain dynamic and responsive to the ever-changing political landscape.

Finally, effective advocacy requires persistence and resilience. The struggle for human rights and social justice often encounters significant obstacles, particularly in environments dominated by oligarchies or authoritarian regimes. Advocates must be prepared for setbacks and remain committed to their goals, adapting their strategies as necessary. By fostering a culture of perseverance and solidarity within advocacy movements, individuals can inspire hope and encourage sustained efforts to challenge oppressive systems. Ultimately, the strategies for effective advocacy not only promote immediate change but also contribute to building a healthier society that thrives in the face of adversity.

HUMAN RIGHTS IN TIMES OF ADVERSITY
Understanding Human Rights

Understanding human rights is fundamental to grasping the intricate web of political systems and their profound impact on society. Human rights serve as the bedrock of a just society, delineating the inherent dignity and worth of every individual. They are not merely abstract concepts; they embody the principles of freedom, equality, and justice that underpin democratic governance. By understanding these rights, individuals can recognize the responsibilities of their governments and the ethical obligations that come with power. This awareness equips citizens to advocate for their rights and the rights of others, especially in times of adversity when these rights are most threatened.

In the context of political systems, the distinction between oligarchies and democracies becomes particularly relevant. Oligarchies, by concentrating power in the hands of a few, often undermine human rights and perpetuate economic inequality. The ruling elite may manipulate laws and policies to maintain their dominance while marginalizing dissenting voices. Conversely, democracies, grounded in the protection of human rights, empower citizens to participate actively in political life. This fundamental difference highlights the importance of political education and civic engagement, especially among youth, who are the future guardians of these rights. By fostering a culture of awareness and activism, societies can resist the encroachment of tyranny and ensure that human rights remain at the forefront of political discourse.

The struggle for human rights is particularly poignant in authoritarian regimes, where dissent is often met with suppression. Human rights advocacy in such contexts is not just a noble pursuit; it is a courageous act that can inspire change. Advocates often risk their safety and freedom to shine a light on abuses, calling for accountability and justice. Their efforts underscore the critical role that international organizations play in promoting human rights, providing support and resources to those fighting for dignity and respect in their own countries. These organizations act as beacons of hope, amplifying voices that might otherwise go unheard and fostering a global environment where human rights are recognized and upheld.

Moreover, the relationship between political systems and social justice cannot be overstated. Political structures that prioritize human rights create an environment conducive to social equity and collective well-being. Conversely, systems that neglect these rights often exacerbate divisions and create fertile ground for conflict. By advocating for policies that promote social justice and protect human rights, citizens can challenge the status quo and work towards a society where everyone can thrive. This transformative potential lies within the actions of individuals and communities who refuse to accept injustice and actively seek to create a better future.

In examining historical case studies of tyranny and resistance, we can draw invaluable lessons about the resilience of the human spirit. These stories reveal the profound impact that collective action can have in challenging oppressive regimes and reclaiming human rights. The influence of political organizations in shaping policy and advocating for change has been pivotal in these movements. As we reflect on these narratives, it becomes evident that understanding human rights is not just an academic exercise; it is a crucial element in the ongoing struggle for a just society. By committing to this understanding, we empower ourselves to engage with the political landscape more effectively, ensuring that the principles of justice and equality guide our collective journey toward a brighter future.

SUPPORTING HUMAN RIGHTS DURING CRISES

Supporting human rights during crises is not just a moral imperative; it is a vital cornerstone of a resilient society. Crises, whether they are natural disasters, economic downturns, or political upheavals, can lead to the erosion of human rights as governments often prioritize control over compassion. However, history has shown that these challenging times can also serve as catalysts for change, prompting individuals and organizations to rise in defense of fundamental freedoms. By understanding the political systems that govern our societies, we can better advocate for human rights and create a framework that supports justice and equality for all.

In the face of adversity, it is essential to recognize how oligarchies can exacerbate economic inequality and suppress human rights. These power structures tend to prioritize the interests of a select few at the expense of the broader population. During crises, the voices of those in power often drown out the needs of the marginalized. Therefore, it is crucial for advocates and citizens alike to remain vigilant and challenge these injustices, calling for policies that prioritize human dignity over entrenched interests. The fight for human rights must be proactive, ensuring that the most vulnerable members of society are not left behind.

Human rights advocacy becomes even more critical in authoritarian regimes, where crises can lead to increased repression. In such environments, the pursuit of justice often requires extraordinary courage and creativity. Grassroots movements, international solidarity, and digital activism have emerged as powerful tools for promoting human rights in the face of tyranny. By fostering a culture of civic engagement and political education, we empower individuals to stand against oppression and demand accountability.

Supporting human rights during crises is not merely an act of charity; it is an assertion of our collective humanity and a commitment to a future where everyone can thrive.

The role of international organizations in promoting human rights cannot be overstated. These entities serve as both watchdogs and advocates, amplifying the voices of those who are silenced in their home countries. They provide essential resources, legal frameworks, and platforms for dialogue that can help protect human rights during turbulent times. By supporting these organizations and holding them accountable, we contribute to a global network that prioritizes human dignity. It is a reminder that our struggles are interconnected, and that solidarity across borders is essential in the fight against injustice.

Ultimately, the relationship between political systems and social justice is a dynamic one, shaped by the actions of individuals, organizations, and governments. During crises, we must embrace the opportunity to educate ourselves and others about the importance of human rights. By fostering a culture of awareness and engagement, we can build a society that not only withstands adversity but emerges stronger and more equitable. The journey towards a just world is long and fraught with challenges, but with unwavering commitment and collective action, we can ensure that human rights are upheld and celebrated, even in the darkest of times.

BUILDING RESILIENT COMMUNITIES

Building resilient communities requires a deep understanding of the political systems that shape our lives. In times of adversity, communities that are aware of their political context can mobilize effectively, advocate for their rights, and pressure those in power to heed their voices. This awareness is particularly crucial as we navigate the complexities of oligarchy and tyranny, where power is often concentrated in the hands of a few, leading to economic inequality and human rights abuses. By fostering a politically informed populace, we empower individuals to not only recognize injustices but also to engage actively in the political process, transforming passive observers into proactive advocates for change.

The impact of oligarchic structures on economic inequality cannot be overstated. In communities where wealth and influence are held by a select few, the majority often struggles to access basic resources and opportunities. This disparity breeds frustration and disillusionment, which can erode the social fabric of a community. However, resilient communities can challenge these dynamics by organizing grassroots movements that demand accountability and equitable distribution of resources. By understanding the mechanisms of power and influence, community members can advocate for policies that address systemic inequalities, ensuring that everyone has a stake in the economic landscape.

Human rights advocacy becomes paramount in the face of authoritarian regimes that seek to silence dissent and suppress freedoms. Resilient communities recognize that their strength lies in unity and collective action. By collaborating with local and international organizations committed to human rights, they can amplify their voices and draw attention to abuses. Education plays a vital role in this process; when individuals understand their rights and how to advocate for them, they become empowered agents of change. Consequently, building a culture of political education and civic engagement, especially among youth, lays the groundwork for future generations to continue the fight for justice and equity.

The relationship between political systems and social justice is intricate and vital for the health of any society. Resilient communities understand that social justice is not merely an ideal but a necessity for harmony and progress. By advocating for inclusion and representation within political structures, they challenge the status quo and push for reforms that benefit all members of society. Comparative analyses of different political systems highlight the importance of democratic principles in fostering social justice, revealing that communities thrive best when they participate actively in decision-making processes. This engagement encourages diverse perspectives and solutions, ultimately leading to a more equitable society.

International organizations play a crucial role in promoting human rights and supporting resilient communities facing adversity. By providing resources, expertise, and a global platform for advocacy, these organizations can help local communities amplify their struggles and successes. Historical case studies of tyranny and resistance illustrate the power of solidarity and international attention in dismantling oppressive systems. When communities are equipped with knowledge, resources, and support, they can withstand the pressures of authoritarianism and emerge stronger. Building resilient communities is not just about survival; it is about thriving and ensuring that every voice is heard, every right is upheld, and every individual has the opportunity to contribute to a just and equitable society.

POLITICAL EDUCATION AND CIVIC ENGAGEMENT FOR YOUTH

The Importance of Political Education

Political education serves as the bedrock of a thriving democracy and a catalyst for social progress. In an age where information is abundant yet often misleading, understanding political systems becomes imperative for adults seeking to navigate the complexities of governance and civic life. Political education empowers individuals to discern the nuances between various political organizations, fostering a critical awareness of how these entities influence decision-making and the distribution of power. By grasping the intricacies of systems like oligarchy and tyranny, citizens can better advocate for their rights and the rights of others, ensuring that they remain vigilant against the encroachments of authoritarianism.

The impact of oligarchies on economic inequality is a pressing issue that underscores the necessity of political education. When a small group holds disproportionate power, the wealth gap widens, leading to societal discontent and stagnation. Understanding the mechanisms through which oligarchies operate allows citizens to challenge these structures effectively. By educating themselves about the policies that perpetuate economic disparity, adults can engage in informed discussions and advocate for reforms that promote equity. This awareness not only enhances personal agency but also cultivates a collective effort toward dismantling systemic barriers that hinder social mobility.

Human rights advocacy in authoritarian regimes exemplifies the crucial role of political education in fostering resilience and resistance. Individuals who understand their rights and the global standards of human dignity are better equipped to confront oppression. Political education provides the tools to recognize injustices and mobilize support, both locally and internationally. As adults engage with historical case studies of tyranny and resistance, they gain insights into the strategies that have led to meaningful change. This knowledge inspires a sense of responsibility, urging individuals to participate in movements that champion justice and equality, even amid adversity.

The relationship between political systems and social justice cannot be ignored, as it illustrates the profound influence that governance has on the fabric of society. Political education illuminates the pathways through which social justice can be pursued, highlighting the importance of civic engagement. Adults who are politically educated are more likely to vote, advocate for policy changes, and hold their representatives accountable. This active participation is vital for nurturing a democratic culture that prioritizes human rights and social equity. By fostering a politically aware citizenry, societies can cultivate an environment where justice is not merely an aspiration but a lived reality for all.

International organizations play a pivotal role in promoting human rights, and understanding their functions is essential for adults seeking to engage in global advocacy. Political education equips individuals with the knowledge necessary to navigate the complex landscape of international relations and humanitarian efforts. Awareness of how these organizations operate empowers citizens to support initiatives that uplift marginalized voices and protect fundamental freedoms. By recognizing the interconnectedness of global political systems, adults can contribute to a more just world, championing human rights not only within their own countries but also across borders. This commitment to global solidarity is vital for fostering a healthy society that can thrive, even in challenging times.

ENGAGING YOUTH IN CIVIC LIFE

Engaging youth in civic life is a cornerstone of a thriving democracy, as their active participation shapes the future of political systems and societal structures. Young people today possess a unique perspective on issues that affect their lives and communities. By fostering their engagement in civic matters, we empower them to advocate for human rights, challenge economic inequalities, and resist tyranny. Encouraging youth involvement not only cultivates informed citizens but also nurtures future leaders equipped to confront the complex challenges of our time.

Political education plays a pivotal role in this engagement, providing young individuals with the tools to understand the intricacies of political systems. By exploring concepts such as oligarchy and democracy, youth can grasp the implications of power dynamics and their direct impact on social justice. Educational programs that emphasize critical thinking and analysis of historical case studies illuminate the struggle against tyranny and the importance of resilience in the face of oppression. When young people are educated about their rights and the mechanisms of political change, they become empowered to take action and advocate for a more equitable society.

Civic engagement can take many forms, from participating in local governance to joining advocacy groups focused on human rights. By engaging in community service, youth learn the value of collaboration and the importance of contributing to the common good. Organizations that promote youth involvement in politics, such as youth councils and advocacy networks, provide platforms for young voices to influence policy-making. These initiatives not only help bridge the gap between generations but also ensure that the perspectives of younger citizens are considered in decision-making processes, ultimately leading to more inclusive governance.

The relationship between political systems and the active participation of youth is critical, especially in times of adversity. Authoritarian regimes often suppress youth engagement, fearing the power of a mobilized generation. Conversely, democracies that encourage participation foster resilience and innovation. By equipping young people with the skills to engage in civic life, societies can fortify themselves against the encroachment of oligarchy and tyranny. The vitality of a healthy society is rooted in the commitment of its youth to advocate for justice, equality, and human rights, ensuring that the foundations of democracy remain strong.

International organizations also play a significant role in promoting youth engagement in civic life. By supporting initiatives that empower young people, these organizations foster a global culture of activism and advocacy. Young leaders are inspired to collaborate across borders, drawing strength from shared experiences and aspirations. In this interconnected world, the voices of youth can resonate far beyond their immediate communities. As they engage in civic life, they challenge existing power dynamics, advocate for their rights, and contribute to a global movement for social justice, shaping a future that reflects their values and dreams.

TOOLS FOR EMPOWERING FUTURE LEADERS

In the quest to empower future leaders, it is essential to provide them with the tools that not only enhance their understanding of political systems but also cultivate their ability to effect meaningful change. Political education serves as the cornerstone of this empowerment, equipping individuals with the knowledge necessary to navigate the complexities of governance, engage in civic life, and advocate for human rights. By fostering an environment where political literacy is prioritized, we prepare future leaders to challenge oppressive structures and champion the principles of justice and equality.

Understanding the dynamics of power is critical in addressing the challenges posed by oligarchies and authoritarian regimes. Future leaders must be armed with the analytical skills to dissect how these systems perpetuate economic inequality and undermine democratic values. By studying historical case studies of tyranny and resistance, they can draw inspiration from those who have bravely stood against oppression. This historical insight not only informs their understanding of past struggles but also ignites a passion for activism that can drive societal change today.

The importance of civic engagement cannot be overstated in this context. Future leaders should be encouraged to participate actively in their communities, understanding that grassroots movements are often the heartbeat of social change. Political organizations play a vital role in this ecosystem, as they mobilize citizens and influence policy-making. By fostering partnerships between emerging leaders and established organizations, we can create a collaborative framework where innovative ideas flourish, and collective action becomes a powerful tool for social justice.

Moreover, the role of international organizations in promoting human rights cannot be overlooked. Future leaders must be educated about the global landscape of human rights advocacy and the mechanisms through which international bodies hold governments accountable. This knowledge empowers them to advocate not only for their local communities but also for marginalized groups on a global scale. By understanding the interconnectedness of political systems, they can effectively contribute to a world where human rights are universally respected and upheld.

In conclusion, empowering future leaders requires a multifaceted approach that encompasses political education, civic engagement, historical awareness, and an understanding of international advocacy. By providing these essential tools, we equip them to navigate the complexities of political systems, challenge injustice, and foster a society where human rights thrive. The journey may be fraught with challenges, but with determination and the right resources, future leaders can emerge as beacons of hope and catalysts for positive change in a world that desperately needs their vision and leadership.

POLITICAL SYSTEMS AND SOCIAL JUSTICE
The Interconnection of Politics and Justice

The intricate relationship between politics and justice forms the bedrock of any thriving society. When political systems are structured to prioritize justice, they foster an environment where human rights are upheld, and citizens feel empowered to participate in governance. Conversely, when politics becomes a tool for oppression, it spirals into tyranny and oligarchy, creating systems that perpetuate inequality and injustice. Understanding this interconnection is crucial, as it not only informs the way we navigate the complex landscape of power dynamics but also guides our commitment to advocating for a society where justice prevails.

In oligarchies, wealth and power become concentrated in the hands of a few, leading to stark economic inequalities that undermine the foundational principles of justice. The decisions made by political organizations often reflect the interests of the elite rather than the broader populace, resulting in policies that marginalize the vulnerable. This concentration of power disenfranchises citizens, stripping them of their agency and making justice an abstract concept rather than a lived reality. To combat this, it is vital to promote political education and civic engagement, empowering individuals to challenge the status quo and advocate for equitable policies that serve the common good.

Human rights advocacy plays an essential role in countering the adverse effects of authoritarian regimes. In environments where dissent is stifled and freedoms are curtailed, courageous individuals and organizations emerge as beacons of hope, championing the cause of justice against overwhelming odds. Their efforts not only highlight the pervasive violations of human rights but also inspire collective action and resilience among citizens. Supporting these advocates is paramount, as their work lays the groundwork for future generations to inherit a society where justice is not just an ideal but a tangible reality.

International organizations have a crucial part to play in promoting human rights and fostering justice across borders. They serve as watchdogs, holding governments accountable for their actions and providing the necessary support to those fighting against oppression. By facilitating dialogue, offering resources, and amplifying the voices of marginalized communities, these organizations contribute to a global culture of justice that transcends national boundaries. Their efforts underscore the interconnectedness of political systems, illustrating that the pursuit of justice is not confined to one nation but is a universal endeavor.

Historical case studies of tyranny and resistance exemplify the enduring struggle for justice within political systems. They remind us that while oppressive regimes may rise, the human spirit's resilience often leads to transformative change. By examining these narratives, we gain valuable insights into the mechanics of power and resistance, equipping ourselves with the knowledge to navigate current challenges. As we reflect on the interconnection of politics and justice, we are called to action, inspired to create a society where the ideals of equity, freedom, and justice flourish even in the face of adversity.

SOCIAL JUSTICE MOVEMENTS AROUND THE WORLD

Social justice movements across the globe have emerged as powerful catalysts for change, challenging entrenched systems of inequality and advocating for the rights of marginalized communities. From the streets of Hong Kong to the neighborhoods of Ferguson, these movements embody the resilience and determination of individuals who refuse to accept the status quo. They highlight the urgent need for a deep understanding of political systems and the impact these structures have on the lives of ordinary people. As citizens engage in the struggle for justice, they illuminate the intricate relationship between political advocacy and the pursuit of human rights.

In many countries, social justice movements have risen in response to oppressive regimes and policies that perpetuate economic inequality. The Arab Spring serves as a poignant example, where citizens united to demand democratic reforms and an end to governmental tyranny. These movements not only sought political change but also aimed to dismantle the oligarchies that had concentrated wealth and power in the hands of a few. As individuals mobilize, they create networks of solidarity that empower communities to challenge systemic injustices, demonstrating that collective action can reshape the political landscape and foster a more equitable society.

Human rights advocacy plays a crucial role in these movements, particularly in authoritarian regimes where dissent is often met with severe repercussions. Activists and organizations work tirelessly to shine a light on abuses, using both local and international platforms to amplify their voices. The role of international organizations, such as the United Nations and Amnesty International, cannot be overstated. They provide vital support to grassroots movements, offering resources, visibility, and pressure on oppressive governments to respect human rights. This collaboration underscores the importance of global solidarity in the fight for justice, reminding us that the struggle for human rights transcends borders.

Political education and civic engagement are fundamental for nurturing the next generation of activists and leaders. By equipping youth with the knowledge of their rights and the workings of political systems, we empower them to become informed advocates for change. The ability to critically analyze the impact of oligarchies and democracies on social justice movements is essential in fostering a politically aware populace. As young people engage in these discussions, they not only challenge existing power dynamics but also envision a future where equity and justice are central to societal progress.

The historical context of tyranny and resistance provides invaluable lessons for contemporary movements. Case studies of past social justice struggles reveal patterns of resilience and innovation that can inform current efforts. By understanding the successes and failures of those who came before us, we can refine our strategies and build upon their legacies. The interplay between political organizations and policy-making highlights the need for strategic alliances in the pursuit of social justice. Together, these elements create a tapestry of activism, each thread contributing to a larger narrative that champions the rights of all individuals, fostering a society where justice prevails even in the face of adversity.

CREATING EQUITABLE POLITICAL SYSTEMS

Creating equitable political systems is essential for fostering a society where every individual has the opportunity to thrive. At the heart of this endeavor lies the understanding that political systems shape not only governance but also the very fabric of our communities. By promoting inclusivity and empowering marginalized voices, we can dismantle the structures that perpetuate inequality and injustice. An equitable political system encourages participation from all segments of society, ensuring that decisions reflect the diverse needs and aspirations of the populace.

In confronting the challenges posed by oligarchy and tyranny, it is crucial to recognize the impact these systems have on economic inequality. Wealth concentration within a small elite not only stifles economic mobility but also undermines democratic principles. To combat this, we must advocate for policies that promote wealth redistribution and equitable access to resources. By creating political frameworks that prioritize the welfare of all citizens, rather than a privileged few, we can nurture environments where economic opportunities are shared, thus fostering a healthier society capable of weathering adversity.

Human rights advocacy is particularly vital in authoritarian regimes where dissent is often met with repression. The fight for equity cannot be won in silence; it requires courageous individuals and organizations willing to challenge oppressive systems. By championing human rights and holding governments accountable, we contribute to a culture of justice that transcends borders. This advocacy not only supports those living under authoritarian rule but also reinforces global norms that protect individual freedoms and dignity, thereby creating a more equitable international landscape.

Political education and civic engagement are fundamental in cultivating a politically aware and active citizenry, especially among youth. By equipping young people with the knowledge of their rights and the tools to engage in political processes, we empower them to be agents of change. Encouraging dialogue around social justice and systemic inequality helps to foster empathy and understanding, creating a generation that values equity as a cornerstone of their societal engagement. This proactive approach ensures that future leaders are committed to sustaining and enhancing equitable political systems.

The role of international organizations in promoting human rights cannot be overlooked in the quest for equitable political systems. These entities serve as watchdogs, advocates, and platforms for collaboration among nations striving for justice. By supporting initiatives that prioritize human rights and social equity, international organizations can help mitigate the effects of oligarchic and tyrannical governance. Through comparative analyses of political systems, we gain valuable insights into best practices and innovative approaches that can be adapted to different contexts, ultimately guiding us toward the establishment of fair and just political environments that empower all members of society.

THE ROLE OF INTERNATIONAL ORGANIZATIONS
How International Organizations Promote Human Rights

International organizations play a pivotal role in the promotion of human rights, acting as watchdogs and advocates on the global stage. They serve as platforms for dialogue and cooperation among nations, working to ensure that the fundamental rights of individuals are recognized and protected. Through their efforts, they help to establish international norms and standards that guide member states in their treatment of citizens. These organizations, such as the United Nations, Amnesty International, and Human Rights Watch, not only monitor human rights abuses but also mobilize resources and support for individuals and groups fighting for their rights in oppressive regimes.

One of the keyways international organizations promote human rights is through the establishment of legal frameworks and treaties that bind countries to uphold specific standards. Instruments like the Universal Declaration of Human Rights and various international covenants create a foundation for accountability, providing a reference point for advocacy efforts. These documents articulate the rights and freedoms that every individual is entitled to, and they empower activists and organizations to hold governments accountable when they fail to comply. This legal backing fosters an environment where human rights can be recognized as universal, transcending cultural and political boundaries.

Moreover, international organizations engage in capacity-building initiatives that empower local communities and civil society organizations. By providing training, resources, and technical assistance, they equip individuals with the tools necessary to advocate for their rights effectively. This grassroots approach is particularly crucial in authoritarian regimes where local voices are often silenced. By strengthening local advocacy efforts, international organizations create a ripple effect, amplifying the voices of those who might otherwise be ignored. This empowerment not only aids immediate human rights struggles but also fosters a culture of civic engagement and political activism that can thrive even in challenging environments.

In times of crisis, international organizations are often at the forefront of humanitarian responses, providing protection and assistance to vulnerable populations. Their ability to mobilize quickly and efficiently can make a significant difference in the lives of those affected by conflict, persecution, or natural disasters. Through advocacy campaigns, they raise awareness of human rights violations and generate pressure on governments to act. This response is critical in fostering a sense of global solidarity, reminding us that human rights are not just a local concern but a shared responsibility that calls for collective action.

Finally, the influence of international organizations extends beyond immediate interventions; they play a significant role in shaping the global discourse on human rights. By promoting principles of justice, equality, and dignity, they challenge the status quo and inspire movements for change. Their work encourages individuals and communities to envision a world where human rights are universally respected, motivating citizens to engage in the political process. As we navigate the complexities of modern political systems, understanding the impact of these organizations is essential in fostering a society where human rights are upheld, ensuring that we collectively thrive even in the face of adversity.

THE IMPACT OF GLOBAL GOVERNANCE

The impact of global governance on society is profound, shaping not only the political landscape but also influencing economic stability, social justice, and individual rights. In an interconnected world, the decisions made by international organizations, coalitions, and treaties resonate far beyond borders, creating a framework within which nations interact. The role of global governance is particularly critical in addressing issues of human rights and economic inequality, where collective action can foster environments that promote equity and justice. By understanding how these systems operate, individuals can better appreciate their importance in supporting a healthy society, especially during times of adversity.

Global governance serves as an essential mechanism for promoting human rights, especially in authoritarian regimes where such principles may be systematically violated. International organizations, such as the United Nations, play a pivotal role in advocating for human rights standards and holding governments accountable. Through various treaties and conventions, these organizations provide a platform for dialogue and action, empowering citizens and civil society to demand their rights. The influence of global governance in this realm highlights the interconnectedness of local struggles and international support, illustrating how individuals can unite across borders to challenge tyranny and promote justice.

The relationship between political systems and economic inequality cannot be overlooked in the discourse on global governance. Oligarchies, characterized by the concentration of power in the hands of a few, often exacerbate disparities within societies. Through comparative analysis, we can observe how the lack of democratic engagement and accountability leads to policies that favor elite interests at the expense of the broader population. In contrast, democratic governance models, when supported by robust global frameworks, can create more equitable economic opportunities and foster inclusive growth. This understanding encourages individuals to advocate for political systems that prioritize social justice and economic equity.

Political education and civic engagement are critical components in the fight against injustice and inequality. By equipping youth with the knowledge and tools to navigate political landscapes, we cultivate a generation that is not only aware of their rights but also empowered to advocate for them. Global governance initiatives often emphasize the importance of education in fostering civic responsibility and engagement. When young people understand the dynamics at play within their political systems and the importance of their voices, they become active participants in shaping a society that values human rights and social equity.

In conclusion, the impact of global governance is far-reaching, influencing political, economic, and social structures worldwide. As we navigate the complexities of our interconnected world, it becomes imperative to understand the mechanisms of power that govern our societies. By engaging with these systems, advocating for human rights, and promoting civic education, individuals can contribute to a healthier, more just society. The challenges of our time call for collective action, and through global governance, we can harness the power of unity to overcome adversity and build a brighter future for all.

COLLABORATIONS FOR CHANGE

Collaborations for change are essential in navigating the complex landscape of political systems. As societies face the challenges of oligarchy and tyranny, the power of collective action emerges as a beacon of hope. Individuals and organizations must unite, leveraging their unique strengths to address the pressing issues of economic inequality and human rights abuses. By fostering alliances that bridge diverse sectors of society, from grassroots movements to international organizations, we can create a formidable front against oppressive regimes and advocate for a more just world.

In understanding the impact of oligarchy on economic inequality, it becomes clear that collaboration is not just beneficial but necessary. Oligarchs often consolidate wealth and power, marginalizing the voices of the disenfranchised. By coming together, advocates, activists, and community leaders can amplify their message, drawing attention to the systemic injustices that perpetuate inequality. Collaborative efforts can lead to innovative solutions that empower individuals, promote economic equity, and dismantle the barriers erected by those in power.

Human rights advocacy thrives on collaboration, particularly in authoritarian regimes where dissent is often met with severe repercussions. Organizations that work in solidarity with local activists can provide critical support, whether through resources, training, or international attention. These collaborations can be pivotal in creating safe spaces for dialogue, fostering resilience among communities, and mobilizing global networks to challenge oppressive practices. When united, the voices advocating for human rights become a chorus that demands accountability and change.

Political education and civic engagement form the bedrock of any successful collaboration for change. By equipping youth with the knowledge of political systems and the importance of civic participation, we foster a generation that is not only aware of their rights but also empowered to advocate for them. Collaborative educational initiatives that engage schools, universities, and community organizations can inspire young people to take an active role in shaping their societies. When youth understand the dynamics of power and the significance of their involvement, they become catalysts for transformative change.

International organizations play a crucial role in promoting human rights by fostering global collaboration. These entities connect local movements, facilitating the exchange of strategies, resources, and knowledge. By analyzing historical case studies of tyranny and resistance, we can learn from the past and develop more effective strategies for dismantling structures of oppression and building a more just and equitable world.

THE PATH TO FREEDOM

The journey toward freedom is often fraught with challenges, yet it is a path illuminated by the courage of those who have walked it before us. Understanding political systems is not merely an academic exercise; it is a vital endeavor that empowers individuals to navigate the complexities of their societies. As we delve into the intricate dynamics of power, we uncover the mechanisms through which oligarchies and tyrannies operate, revealing the ways in which they can stifle human rights and perpetuate economic inequality. The freedom we seek is intertwined with our ability to recognize these systems and their impacts on our lives, driving us toward a collective awakening.

In the face of adversity, the importance of human rights advocacy becomes ever more pronounced. Authoritarian regimes often suppress dissent, yet history shows us that resistance springs from the belief in fundamental freedoms. This belief can galvanize citizens, fostering a culture of activism that demands accountability and justice. By championing human rights, we not only confront tyranny but also lay the groundwork for a healthier society, one where dignity is upheld and the voices of the marginalized are amplified. Each act of advocacy becomes a steppingstone on the path to liberation, demonstrating that change is possible when individuals unite around shared values.

Political education and civic engagement are crucial pillars in nurturing the next generation of leaders and activists. By equipping youth with the knowledge of political systems and the significance of their participation, we empower them to become informed citizens capable of influencing change. The relationship between political systems and social justice is profound; when individuals are educated about their rights and the mechanisms of power, they are better prepared to challenge injustices. Encouraging active participation fosters a sense of responsibility and agency, inspiring young people to contribute to a society that prioritizes equity and inclusivity.

International organizations play an indispensable role in promoting human rights across the globe. They serve as watchdogs, holding governments accountable and providing support to local movements championing justice. By facilitating dialogue and cooperation among nations, these organizations help to create an environment where human rights are respected and upheld. The influence of international bodies in advocating for oppressed populations highlights the interconnectedness of our struggles; freedom in one part of the world can inspire movements in another. This global solidarity reinforces the idea that the fight for liberty transcends borders.

Comparative analyses of oligarchies and democracies reveal the stark contrasts in how power is wielded and its implications for society. Historical case studies of tyranny and resistance showcase the resilience of the human spirit in the face of oppression. Each narrative serves as a reminder that the path to freedom is not linear, but rather a tapestry woven with both triumphs and setbacks. As we reflect on these experiences, we recognize our role in shaping the future. By understanding the dynamics of power and actively engaging in our communities, we contribute to a legacy of freedom that honors those who fought for it before us, paving the way for generations to come.

THE INFLUENCE OF POLITICAL ORGANIZATIONS ON POLICY MAKING
Understanding Policy Formulation

Policy formulation is a critical process in the functioning of any political system, shaping the laws and guidelines that govern society. Understanding how policies are created allows individuals to engage meaningfully with their government and advocate for changes that reflect their values and needs. At the heart of policy formulation lies a complex interplay of political organizations, public opinion, and the overarching political system. Engaging with this process equips citizens with the tools to influence decisions that affect their lives, fostering a more informed and active populace capable of challenging the status quo.

In democratic societies, policy formulation often begins with extensive debates within political organizations, where diverse perspectives are considered and negotiated. This participatory approach ensures that a variety of voices are heard, reflecting the interests of different societal groups. However, in oligarchies, the process can become skewed, favoring the elite while silencing the majority. Recognizing this disparity is crucial for advocating for policies that address economic inequality and promote social justice. By understanding how power dynamics shape policy outcomes, individuals can better navigate and challenge the structures that perpetuate injustice.

Human rights advocacy plays a vital role in policy formulation, particularly in authoritarian regimes where dissent is often met with repression. Advocates strive to bring attention to violations and push for reforms that uphold fundamental freedoms.

Understanding the mechanisms of policy formulation in these contexts enables advocates to craft strategies that resonate with both local populations and the international community. A well-informed citizenry can mobilize support for human rights initiatives, fostering a culture of accountability and transparency in governance, even in the face of adversity.

Political education and civic engagement are essential components of a healthy society, empowering youth to participate actively in the policy-making process. By instilling an understanding of political systems and the importance of advocacy from an early age, young people can become catalysts for change, challenging oligarchic structures and advocating for their rights. This engagement not only enhances their knowledge but also builds a sense of responsibility towards their communities, ensuring that future generations continue the fight for equity and justice.

International organizations play a pivotal role in promoting human rights and influencing policy formulation on a global scale. Through comparative analyses of different political systems, these organizations provide valuable insights into the best practices and strategies that can be employed to support democratic governance. By collaborating with local political organizations, they can help amplify the voices of marginalized communities, ensuring that policy formulation is inclusive and reflective of the diverse needs of society. Together, these efforts can pave the way for a more equitable world, where policies are crafted with the intention of uplifting all individuals, particularly in times of adversity.

THE ROLE OF LOBBYING AND ADVOCACY GROUPS

Lobbying and advocacy groups play a pivotal role in shaping political landscapes and influencing policy decisions, often acting as conduits between the public and those in power. These organizations operate under the premise that diverse voices should be heard in the halls of governance, advocating for a range of issues from human rights to environmental protection. Their efforts can lead to substantial changes in legislation and public policy, often elevating the concerns of marginalized communities that might otherwise go unnoticed. Through strategic communication and mobilization, these groups not only raise awareness but also empower citizens to engage with their political systems, ensuring that democracy remains vibrant and responsive.

The significance of lobbying is particularly pronounced in the context of economic inequality, where oligarchies can stifle the voices of the many in favor of a privileged few. Advocacy groups often emerge as champions for equitable policies, fighting against the entrenched interests that perpetuate disparity. By leveraging research, grassroots movements, and coalition-building, these organizations challenge the status quo and push for reforms that promote social justice. Their work highlights the interconnectedness of political systems and economic outcomes, demonstrating how advocacy can serve as a powerful counterbalance to the influence of wealth in politics.

In authoritarian regimes, human rights advocacy takes on an even more urgent role, as these environments often suppress dissent and curtail freedoms. Advocacy groups become lifelines for those who dare to speak out against oppression, using international platforms to amplify their struggles. Through lobbying efforts, they can bring global attention to human rights violations, mobilizing support from international organizations and foreign governments. This transnational solidarity is crucial in pressuring authoritarian regimes to adhere to fundamental human rights standards, showcasing how advocacy can foster resilience in the face of tyranny.

Political education and civic engagement are essential components of a healthy society, particularly for youth who will inherit the challenges of tomorrow. Advocacy groups play a vital role in equipping young people with the knowledge and tools necessary to navigate complex political systems. By promoting awareness and involvement, these organizations inspire future generations to become active participants in democracy. This engagement not only nurtures informed citizens but also fosters a culture of accountability, where individuals recognize their power to effect change and advocate for their rights and the rights of others.

Finally, the comparative analysis of oligarchies and democracies reveals the crucial impact of political organizations on policy-making processes. Lobbying and advocacy groups often serve as the bridge between citizens and their representatives, translating public needs into actionable policies. In democratic contexts, these organizations can thrive, fostering an environment where multiple perspectives are considered and debated. Conversely, in oligarchic systems, the concentration of power can stifle such discourse, leading to policies that reflect the interests of a select few. Understanding the dynamics of these groups provides insight into the broader mechanisms of power, illustrating the essential role they play in advocating for a just and equitable society amidst the challenges of modern governance.

CASE STUDIES OF INFLUENTIAL POLITICAL ORGANIZATIONS

The study of influential political organizations reveals profound insights into the mechanisms of power and the impact they wield over society. One notable example is the National Democratic Institute (NDI), which has played a pivotal role in promoting democratic governance worldwide. By focusing on strengthening civic engagement and enhancing the capabilities of political institutions, the NDI exemplifies how political organizations can foster resilience in communities facing adversity. Their initiatives in countries transitioning from authoritarian rule demonstrate that empowering citizens to participate in the political process can lead to tangible improvements in governance and human rights.

Another compelling case is the American Civil Liberties Union (ACLU), which has consistently championed civil rights and liberties in the United States. The ACLU's advocacy against governmental overreach serves as a testament to the importance of protecting individual freedoms in the face of potential tyranny. Their legal battles have not only influenced public policy but have also inspired countless individuals to engage in civic activism. This highlights the critical role political organizations play in defending human rights and ensuring that marginalized voices are heard, fostering a society where justice prevails.

The international organization Human Rights Watch (HRW) offers a powerful example of how advocacy can challenge oppressive regimes. By documenting human rights abuses and holding governments accountable, HRW plays a crucial role in raising global awareness and mobilizing support for those suffering under tyrannical rule. Their work emphasizes the interconnectedness of global politics, illustrating how international organizations can influence domestic policies and encourage systemic change. The case of HRW underscores the importance of solidarity and collective action in the fight for human dignity.

In the realm of economic inequality, the Economic Policy Institute (EPI) stands out for its research and advocacy aimed at addressing the disparities exacerbated by oligarchic structures. EPI's focus on the correlation between wealth concentration and political power offers critical insights into how oligarchies can undermine social equity. By equipping citizens with data-driven analysis, EPI empowers them to engage in informed discussions about economic justice, thus fostering a more equitable society. Their efforts illustrate that understanding the political landscape is essential for addressing systemic inequalities and advocating for policies that benefit all.

Lastly, the Youth Empowerment Project (YEP) is a remarkable case study showcasing the importance of political education and civic engagement among younger generations. Through workshops and community initiatives, YEP instills a sense of agency in youth, preparing them to navigate and influence the political systems that govern their lives. This organization exemplifies how nurturing informed and active citizens is vital for the sustainability of democracy. As history has shown, the most resilient societies are those where individuals understand their rights and responsibilities, actively participating in the political process to shape a just future for all.

RebELLE Publishing Agency
Chicago, IL, USA